D0604672

MAURITANIA

Ettagale Blauer & Jason Lauré

 **Marshall Cavendish**
Benchmark

New York

PICTURE CREDITS

Cover photo: © Philippe Renault/Hemis/Corbis
Anthony Ham/ Lonely Planet Images: 98, 109, 110 • Jonathan Blair/ National Geographic Images: 53, 119 •AFP/Getty Images: 31 • alt.type/Reuters: 43 • Amro Maraghil/AFP/Getty Images: 117 • Audrius Tomonis: 135 • Barry Iverson//Time Life Pictures/ Getty Images: 37 • Damien Meyer/AFP/Getty Images: 41, 120, 122, 123 • David Boyer/ National Geographic Images: 102 • Don Emmert/AFP/Getty Images: 129 • Eric Wheater/Lonely Planet Images: 4 • Frans Lemmens/ Lonely Planet Images: 71 • G Diana/ AFP/Getty Images: 12 • Georg Gerster/ National Geographic Images: 50 • Georges Gobet/AFP/Getty Images: 15, 40, 42, 44, 46, 74 • Gero Breloer/dpa/Corbis: 70 • Getty Images: 58 • Jane Sweeny/Lonely Planet Images: 21, 80, 100 • Jason Laure: 60, 62, 79, 82, 89, 90, 94 • Jonathan Blair/Corbis: 118 • Lauren Gelfand/AFP/Getty Images: 128 • Malcolm Linton/Liaison/ Getty Images: 73 Margaret Courtney-Clarke/CORBIS: 108 • Mehdi Fedouach/AFP/Getty Images: 95 • Olivier Cirendini/ Lonely Planet Images: 10, 11, 69, 105, 127 • Paul Dymond/ Lonely Planet Images: 83, 103 • photolibrary.com: 1, 3, 5, 6, 7, 8, 9, 14, 17, 18, 19, 22, 23, 26, 57, 59, 65, 67, 78, 91, 99, 104, 114, 116, 124, 125, 130, 131 • Scott Peterson/Liaison/Getty Images: 35 • Sean Gallup/Getty Images: 111 • Seyllou/AFP/Getty Images: 48, 51, 55, 84, 113 • Steve McCurry/ National Geographic Images: 20, 38, 126

PRECEDING PAGE

Two Mauritanian girls.

Publisher (U.S.): Michelle Bisson
Editors: Christine Florie, Stephanie Pee
Copyreader: Daphne Hougham
Designer: Lock Hong Liang
Cover picture researcher: Connie Gardner
Picture researcher: Thomas Khoo

Marshall Cavendish Benchmark
99 White Plains Road
Tarrytown, NY 10591
Web site: www.marshallcavendish.us

© Times Media Private Limited 1997
© Marshall Cavendish International (Asia) Private Limited 2009
® "Cultures of the World" is a registered trademark of Times Publishing Limited.

Originated and designed by Times Media Private Limited
An imprint of Marshall Cavendish International (Asia) Private Limited
A member of Times Publishing Limited.

Marshall Cavendish is a trademark of Times Publishing Limited.

All Internet sites were correct and accurate at the time of printing. All monetary figures in this publication are in U.S. dollars.

Library of Congress Cataloging-in-Publication Data
Blauer, Ettagale.
  Mauritania / by Ettagale Blauer and Jason Lauré
    p. cm. (Cultures of the world)
  Summary: "Provides comprehensive information on the geography, history, governmental structure, economy, cultural diversity, peoples, religion, and culture of Mauritania."—Provided by publisher.
  Includes bibliographical references and index.
  ISBN 978-0-7614-3116-9
1. Mauritania—Juvenile literature. I. Lauré, Jason. II. Title.

DT554.22.B58 2009
966.1—dc22   2007043897

Printed in China
7 6 5 4 3 2 1

CONTENTS

A camel caravan in the Adrar region.

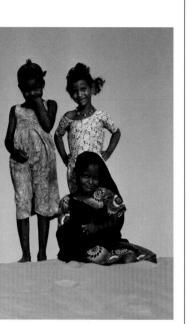

Three young girls sit on the ridge of a sand dune.

4

INTRODUCTION

MAURITANIA IS A COUNTRY WHERE life is ordered by the Sahara and where the camel is the most dependable form of transportation. Although it is one of the least-known countries in the world, it has a rich history. More than 1,000 years ago, Islamic civilization reached Mauritania and played a major role in its development. The country was ruled by France until independence in 1960, and the French influence can still be felt in many areas of life there today.

Nearly half a century after independence, the country is struggling with poverty. The encroaching Sahara overruns more and more of the land every year. Only half the adults can read and write. With the recent discovery of oil, however, the sleepy economy is beginning to wake up. The president, newly elected in 2007, has announced his plans to improve the country's development and to make life somewhat easier for all Mauritanians.

GEOGRAPHY

DESERT, DESERT, AND MORE desert! The Sahara, a desert that stretches across most of northern Africa, takes up three-quarters of Mauritania's total land area. Mauritania is situated in northwest Africa and shares its borders with three countries and a territory called the Western Sahara. The Western Sahara is claimed by Morocco. Mauritania's smallest border is with Algeria, in the northeast. Its entire eastern border as well as more than half of its southern border is shared with Mali. The Senegal River divides the rest of the southern border from the country of Senegal. The western border lies on the Atlantic Ocean, giving the country a shoreline measuring about 435 miles (700 km). Most of this coastline is too rugged for boats to reach the shore. A tiny peninsula in the extreme southwest corner, Cap Blanc, is shared with the Western Sahara.

Above: **A sunrise along Mauritania's coast.**

Opposite: **A large part of Mauritania's landscape is made up of the Sahara.**

LANDSCAPE OF MAURITANIA

Mauritania stretches 1,650 miles (2,655 km) at its widest point from east to west and about 1,800 miles (2,900 km) from north to south. Its total area measures 397,955 square miles (1,030,700 sq km), an area about three times the size of the state of New Mexico. The landscape has been compared to that of the moon because it is marked by deep, dry gorges and rocky sections that rise up. The desert region is mostly flatlands that have eroded over time. Some peaks remain, cropping up abruptly from the desert. The highest peak is Kediet Ijill, near the town of Zouerat. It measures 3,280 feet (1,000 m) in height.

7

Adrar, one of the highest plateau regions, measures more than 1,640 feet (500 m) and is home to the towns of Chinguetti and Ouadane. Adrar is a vast stretch of desert in the center of the country. Within it is the Guelb er Richat, a sunken landmass that measures 25 miles (40 km) in width.

In the center of Mauritania, huge dune ridges create a natural partition that extends across the entire territory from the southwest to the northeast.

In the northern part of Mauritania, the desert becomes sandier and rolling sand dunes begin to appear. Today, the entire region is becoming drier and the desert is advancing slowly to the south. As the land dries up, more and more nomads are forced into the cities. Their livestock have nothing to eat and drink and will die. Without livestock, the people have no transportation and no food. Without food and transportation they must move into the city, where many struggle to adapt to a new way of life.

The Adrar is one of the highest plateau regions.

GEOGRAPHIC ZONES

Mauritania has four geographic and climate zones. These are the Saharan Zone, the Sahelian Zone, the Senegal River Valley, and the Coastal Zone. These zones, or areas, are not rigid divisions. Rather, they merge into each other, with the boundaries shifting over time.

SAHARAN ZONE As the land grows hotter and drier, the Saharan Zone grows even bigger. Today it covers the northern two-thirds of the country. This is the hottest part of Mauritania, but it is also the area where the temperatures may range as much 86°F (30°C) in one day. When the sun goes down, there is no vegetation to trap the heat, so the temperature drops sharply. During the more comfortable months of December and January, the temperature may start at freezing point in the morning at

The harsh conditions of the desert make it difficult for many plants to survive.

CAMELS

Without the camel, people would not have been able to cross the desert. A camel can travel for five to seven days without needing food or water. It can also eat almost anything, including thorny bushes. The camel's broad, flat feet have just two large toes that spread out when it walks, keeping it from sinking into the sand. When a camel walks, it seems to roll from side to side. For this reason, and because it seems to "sail" over the sand, it is often called the ship of the desert. Camel's eyes are protected by two eyelids. The inner lid is translucent, allowing the camels to see where it is going, while still being protected against blowing sand during a sandstorm. Double rows of eyelashes also help keep the sand out of its eyes. The camel used traditionally in the Sahara is the one-hump dromedary. Its milk provides a highly nutritious source of food. There is also a two-hump variety known as the Bactrian camel. A camel can carry a load of 600 pounds (272 kg) quite easily, making it ideal for transportation across the desert. Its long legs also allow it to cross great distances most efficiently at a steady 3 miles an hour (4.8 km per hour).

32°F (0°C) and rise to a high of 100–104°F (38–40°C) by the middle of the afternoon. In the summer months of May, June, and July, the temperature can range from 61°F (16°C) in the morning and soar to 120–122°F (49–50°C) in the afternoon. For more than six months of the year, the average daytime temperature is about 100°F (38°C).

Although there is almost no rainfall in this region, there are some springs and wells. In those areas there is little vegetation. Very small plants and scrub grasses grow there, which are eaten by camels. Although it may not have rained for several years, the seeds of these desert plants remain dormant. When it rains, they spring to life, spreading color across the dunes.

The Saharan sun bakes the land and also dries out the moisture in a person's body. Perspiring drains the body of water, even at rest. This water must be replaced or the body will start to dehydrate. Without water, dizziness and fatigue set in and the ability to think clearly diminishes. At this stage confused travelers may wander off. They are not likely to survive without immediate help in this climate.

The euphorbia is one of the only plants that is able to survive in the Sahara.

SAHELIAN ZONE   South of the Saharan Zone lies a slightly more comfortable region called the Sahelian Zone. There the Sahara gives way to dunes that are covered with scrub grass and acacia trees. Farther to the south, increased rainfall yields yet more vegetation, and the land hardens and turns from sand to clay. This has been the area where nomadic people usually have lived. They can find enough grazing for their camels, cattle, and smaller livestock by moving from time to time, depending on the arrival of the annual rains. If the rains arrive late, perhaps in July instead of in June, the herders move wherever they can find new growth. This may take them across the border into neighboring countries. With the continuous drying up of the African landscape, this Sahelian Zone has moved farther south.

SENEGAL RIVER VALLEY ZONE   This zone is the only area in Mauritania that reliably has had enough rainfall to support agriculture. This includes grain crops, vegetables, and legumes, which include peas, lentils, and soybeans. A severe drought or an invasion of hungry

In 2004 locusts destroyed crops in the town of Aleg, which cut Mauritania's food supply by a quarter.

insects, however, can wipe out crops in the entire country. This happened at the end of 2004 when locusts swept across Mauritania. They infested the entire agricultural zone, destroying food crops that fed one-fourth of the population. A drought at the same time destroyed the small plants that cattle grazed on. This region usually depends on the Senegal River for irrigation, the only permanent river over a vast territory that includes all of Mauritania and also extends deep into Senegal. This makes it a lifeline for the Mauritanians. During the rainy season, the river floods its banks, nourishing the soil. This region has cooler temperatures, and the daily rise and fall in temperatures are also less extreme than in the rest of Mauritania. During seasons of heavy rainfall, baobab and gonakie trees may be found here as well as grasses that offer good feed for livestock.

COASTAL ZONE The fourth climatic zone in Mauritania runs along the entire Atlantic Ocean coastline. Two types of wind batter this shore: the harmattan and the trade winds, the *alizé*. The harmattan blows in from the Sahara, while the trade winds arrive over the ocean from the Canary Islands. The result is a very humid atmosphere, but one with more moderate temperatures. There is little rainfall, but the trade winds bring considerable moisture. They also help to reduce the heat that comes from the harmattan, blowing from the interior of the country.

Mauritania's two major cities, Nouakchott and Nouadhibou, are found there. The shore itself is very unfriendly. The crashing surf and unpredictable sandbanks make boating impossible. Rough ocean waves pound against the shore, molding the sandbanks and shifting the outline of the shore. The tiny peninsula called Ras Nouadhibou is home to the only natural harbor, Dakhlet Nouadhibou. All of Mauritania's minerals are shipped out

SENGEGAL RIVER

The Senegal River is the only permanent river in all of Mauritania. It forms roughly half of Mauritania's southern border with Senegal. The Senegal River rises in Guinea and then flows westward through Mali and Senegal before reaching Mauritania's southern border. Most of the country's established farming takes place here. When the river floods its banks, the water replenishes the soil, adding nutrients that are necessary for farming.

from there. Even on the coast, sand dunes dominate the landscape. The only area without sand dunes is the Senegal River Valley Zone.

CLIMATE

In the Mauritanian Sahara there is almost no rainfall throughout the year. In Nouakchott, the capital city located on the Atlantic Ocean, what little rain that falls comes almost entirely in August, often amounting to no more than 4 inches (102 mm). In the region known as the Sahel, near the border with Senegal, a short rainy season occurs from July to September and allows

a narrow strip of land, some 124 miles (200 km) wide, to be farmed. Unfortunately, this strip is growing narrower every year as the Sahara advances southward. During a particularly dry period in the 1980s, the desert grew and moved southward at about 3.73 miles (6 km) a year. This process is called desertification, meaning that more and more land is turning into part of the desert. This pushed each climate zone southward. The desertlike conditions had even reached some areas along the banks of the Senegal River.

Winds play an important role in the lives of the people in this region. Each one is described by a different name. The extreme heat in Mauritania is caused in part by hot winds called *rifi* that blow in from the south.

Women in the village of Barkeol draw water. The climate in Mauritania is getting increasingly drier, meaning that water is scarce.

Along the coast, trade winds called *alizé* blow in from the ocean, making the normal high temperatures on the shoreline about 5 degrees cooler.

The harmattan is a fierce wind that blows throughout the year. It whips up the loose sand from the desert, making it impossible for anyone to see where he or she is traveling. The harmattan sucks up tons of fine sand and carries it out to the ocean. Such a tremendous amount of sand is dropped into the sea this way that it can create dangerous conditions for ships sailing off the coast of Mauritania.

HURRICANES

What does the weather in Mauritania have to do with hurricanes in the United States? Plenty! The hurricanes that batter the seacoast of the southeastern United States and the Gulf of Mexico arrive directly from Mauritania.

The hot Saharan winds that swirl over Mauritania warms up an air mass that is known as a tropical disturbance. This mass of warm air moves westward, meeting the Atlantic Ocean. There it picks up moisture and the energy of the solar heat that was stored in the ocean and mixes it with the warm air. The tropical disturbance now increases in power, fed by this warm, moist air. The moisture acts as fuel for the hurricane, and it continues to pick up energy as it accelerates westward across the Atlantic Ocean.

This huge swirling mass of air becomes a group of thunderstorms. A storm feeds on the warm waters, getting hotter, higher, and faster. As it approaches the first landmass, the hurricane reaches its greatest fury. Hurricanes that form off Mauritania can strike anywhere they first encounter land. The direction is determined by how much cool air the storm encounters, as well as its internal pressure and whether or not there are any land masses in its way.

FLORA

Local types of vegetation vary from zone to zone and include acacias, soapberry trees, capers, and swallowwort. They are usually found in low-lying areas between dunes, where there is the best chance for water to reach the plants.

A small amount of crop cultivation takes place at oases, places where water is found beneath the sand. Local people plant date palms there, which can survive in the harsh climate. Those trees help to shade other crops from the fierce sun.

In the Sahelian Zone, some baobab trees appear, while in the forest regions of Trarza and Brakna, gum-bearing acacia trees flourish. Forests, however, have been reduced to 0.3 percent of the land—that is, less than one-half of 1 percent of all of Mauritania is forested. This small amount decreases every year.

A dramatic drop in the annual rainfall is a major cause of this loss of forest. The Senegal River Valley Zone used to receive an average of 11.8 inches (300 mm) of rainfall per year. That was cut in half by 1990, to an average of just 5.9 inches (150 mm) per year. As rainfall decreases, vegetation and land dry up and the air grows hotter. Dams that were built in the neighboring country of Mali have contributed to Mauritania's loss of water. The result is a much drier, hotter climate—and a land area with much less vegetation and ground cover.

The swallowwort plant.

The collared flycatcher is
now less frequently seen
in Mauritania.

FAUNA

The delta area of the Senegal River Valley was famous for its birdlife. In the 1960s, more than 10,000 nests built by herons, egrets, and cormorants were found in the mangrove and acacia forests of the region. This abundant birdlife has virtually disappeared with the drying up of the region. A few birds have been spotted in the region from time to time, including the sandpiper, the collared flycatcher, and the spectacled warbler. But the lesser flamingo, which used to breed in the region in great numbers, appears to have vanished.

Larger mammals, such as lions, gazelles, and wildcats, used to thrive in the region. Today, however, because of drought as well as overhunting, those animals have disappeared. It has been more than 40 years since a hippopotamus or manatee has been reported. There are still many jackals and hundreds of warthogs in the national parks of Diawling and in the area of Keur Macène, and crocodiles live in Lake Matmata in the region of Tagant.

CITIES

In all of Mauritania there are only two significant cities: Nouakchott and Nouadhibou. Nouakchott is the capital and Nouadhibou is the major port. There are some small towns, but they are little more than villages. Most of the people live in the two major cities and along the arable Senegal River region in the south.

Nouakchott, the capital city of Mauritania, is situated just inland from the Atlantic Ocean. The shoreline itself floods regularly and is not suitable for new construction. The flat land on which the city was built lies at the very edge of the Sahara. Sand dunes can be seen pushing their way toward the city, driven by the winds that gave the town its name, "place of the winds." The government tried to stop this advance by planting 250,000 trees as a barrier against the desert.

The capital city of Mauritania, Nouakchott.

The winds blow from two directions. Hot winds come from the vast Sahara, while cooling winds blow in over the city from the Atlantic. When Nouakchott was named the capital-to-be of Mauritania in 1957, it was but a small village. As the French turned control of Mauritania to the Mauritanians, they also granted loans for the creation of a real capital. It was a formidable challenge. The dunes kept pushing their way into the city, burying paved streets almost as fast as they could be laid down. And, typical for a desert environment, the wells that supplied the city were a very distant 37 miles (60 km) away. The town's single traffic light had very little traffic to control.

Today, largely because drought has forced people into cities, Nouakchott has a population estimated at more than 600,000. Nearly all the buildings in the city are just one-story tall. Many people set their tents up at the

A grid of branches laid in the dunes surrounding Nouakchott attempt to anchor the desert.

edge of town. In a sense, they are still nomads, but ones who no longer have livestock to tend. In the 1960s, more than 80 percent of the people were nomads. Today it is estimated that only 10 percent are. Within two short generations, the country has had to deal with this complete change in its social structure. That change can be seen in the sprawling city of Nouakchott. There, people live in shantytowns called *kébés*. These also sprung up around all the larger towns and even along the roadways. Conditions in the *kébés* are extremely poor, without adequate water or sanitation, and are breeding grounds for disease.

Nouakchott is the largest city in the Sahara. It has lively markets where people buy their goods and also crafts shops where handmade rugs, silver items, and other crafts may be bought.

A desert tent village located on the outskirts of Nouadhibou and Nouakchott.

HISTORY

THE GEOGRAPHY OF MAURITANIA has played a major role in determining when and how people lived in the region. Long ago this region, and much of the Sahara, was green and wet. There were lakes, rivers, and abundant vegetation. The region was full of wildlife, including elephants, rhinoceroses, and hippopotamuses. Rock drawings and arrowheads show that early humans lived and prospered in the region. Then, about 10,000 years ago, there was a dramatic change in the world's climate. The Ice Age ended, and the climate grew warmer. In the period roughly between about 10,000 to 6,000 years ago, farming took place in the area we now know as the Sahara. The continual warming and drying of the region soon made farming unpredictable, and farmers began moving southward.

By about 4000 to 3000 B.C., people had domesticated cattle and were growing millet, yams, and a local type of rice. Food production was

Left: **Rock carvings at El Ghallacuiya in the Adrar region are evidence of early settlers in the region.**

Opposite: **Remains of an ancient city near Oudane.**

dependable enough for the people to live a settled life on the land rather than having to roam in search of food.

In present-day Mauritania, there is evidence that people were living in organized communities from about 1200 B.C. Archaeologists have found remains of stone villages and the bones of domestic animals that show how those people lived.

Sometime around the third century A.D., camels were introduced into Morocco from western Asis. The Berbers, the first modern people to live in the region, made good use of these amazing creatures that were able to travel great distances without needing water. Trading routes were established in Mauritania, bringing in salt, the most highly valued commodity. For the first time, people could preserve food by using salt. This gave them far greater food security. Salt was as highly valued as gold.

With their camels to carry them across the desert, people began to migrate into present-day Mauritania. Wave after wave of immigration occurred, with each new group pushing the established settlers off their territory.

ARRIVAL OF THE BERBERS

The Berbers were the first group of immigrants to arrive in Mauritania. They arrived from the north in the 3rd and 4th centuries. There was a lull before another wave of Berbers arrived during the 7th and 8th centuries. By the 9th century, in order to control a large part of the trans-Saharan trade route, several Berber communities had come together to form the Sanhadja Confederation. A period of warfare and the breakup of this confederation in the 11th century led to the emergence of a fierce religious group known as the Almoravids, who preached Islamic reform.

The Almoravids were remarkably successful in spreading their influence through northern Africa, stretching all the way across the Mediterranean into present-day Spain.

The next wave of immigration in Mauritania took place over several hundred years. Black Africans from strong kingdoms in Ghana, Mali, and Songhai swept over the Berbers. Then Yemeni Arab groups moved in from the north, pushing both the Berbers and the black Africans out of their territory. In time, the Bani Hassan Yemenis became the most important ethnic and cultural group in all of Mauritania. The Berbers fought long and hard to restrain the Arabs from dominating them. The Mauritanian Thirty Years' War, from 1644 to 1674, was the last great battle between these two peoples. When at last the Berbers succumbed, they fell under the complete domination of these warrior Arabs.

MUSLIMS IN SPAIN

The presence of Muslims in southern Spain began in 711 when Moorish soldiers crossed over from Africa to the very tip of the Iberian Peninsula. Their mission was to spread Islam. An army of 10,000 men, led by General Tarik ibn Ziyad, crossed the straits that separate North Africa from southern Europe. They landed near a huge rock outcropping which became known as Djabal Tarik (Tarik's Mountain). That eventually changed to the name it has today, Gibraltar. The distance across the straits at the narrowest point is just 8 miles (13 km).

The Muslim presence in Spain can still be seen in the great buildings they left behind, including the Alhambra near Granada, built in the 13th and 14th centuries. Muslim scientists, architects, and other professional groups were well ahead of the Christians of their time in terms of inventions and discoveries.

As the Berbers were pushed south, they in turn pushed the black Africans toward the Senegal River Basin. The blacks who remained were captured and forced into slavery. They became a servant class, working for the Arab-Berbers.

By 1674 the ancestors of the ethnic groups living in Mauritania today had been channeled into a distinct social structure. They all spoke Hassaniya Arabic, the form of Arabic spoken in that region, and became known as Moors, or Maures.

Throughout this time, camel caravans traveled along trade routes that stretched across great distances in the Sahara. These caravans formed a vital link in transporting goods from as far south as Timbuktu, capital of the Mali Empire, all the way to North Africa. Merchants carried gold and ivory, goods that were desired in the north. In return, they brought back

The present-day city of Chinguetti, which was once a great center for Islamic learning.

copper, cloth, and other goods. Salt, from mines in northern Mauritania that are still being worked today, was a highly desired commodity. The route also allowed slaves to be transported to the coast, where they were shipped abroad.

Great cities blossomed in the desert, including Chinguetti, which would become one of the most important Islamic religious centers. Islam was one of the most lasting elements of the caravan routes.

EUROPEANS REACH MAURITANIA

Although the Almoravids had conquered much of Spain, Mauritania was virtually unknown to Europeans. Mauritania's rough coastline created a natural barrier to most outsiders. But the Portuguese, among the greatest explorers and sailors in the world, were already setting out in their caravels, their light but almost ideal sailing ships, in search of the great wealth they had heard about in the African kingdoms.

In 1441 the Portuguese sailed along the West African coast, reaching Cap Blanc on the northwest tip of Mauritania. They captured 12 Africans and sailed back to Lisbon. The slave trade that in time wrenched millions of Africans from their homes had begun.

In 1455 the Portuguese established a trading post at Arguin, near Cap Blanc. Their original idea was to get rich quickly in the gold trade, but they were not successful. Instead, they started trading slaves, sending them to work on Portuguese sugar plantations on the island of São Tomé, off the west coast of Africa.

The Portuguese did not remain in the area for long. In short order, control of the lucrative trade changed from the Portuguese to the Spanish and then to the Dutch. The French drove out the Dutch in 1678 and established themselves at Saint Louis, at the mouth of the Senegal River.

Various European powers tried to keep control of the region, each for its own benefit and for more than 50 years, the West African coast was under the governance of the British. Finally, in 1815, at the Congress of Vienna, the French were recognized as the rulers of the West African coast, including the entire stretch that is now Mauritania.

THE FRENCH IN WEST AFRICA

During the early 1800s, French contact with West Africa was restricted to the coast, and most of their business was conducted in Senegal. In order to secure their control of the region, the French had to command the area north of the Senegal River. In 1840 the French declared Senegal a permanent French possession and also included the settlements in Mauritania to be part of that claim. Louis Faidherbe, the French governor of Senegal, fought the Oualo Kingdom of Mauritania, and consolidated French control over an area known as a protectorate. Faidherbe ventured far inland and traveled throughout western and southern Mauritania. But the region was not calm and peaceful. Moorish groups had found they could buy weapons from French companies based in Saint Louis, and Europeans became the targets of their attacks. French control was very weak, and the emboldened Moors were determined to reclaim their territory.

The real beginning of French control over Mauritania came in 1901 when Xavier Coppolani set out to make peace among the Moors and bring them under French "protection." He became known as the Pacific Conqueror of the territory, accomplishing the goal of ruling the people without fighting them. The local leaders, Sheikh Sidiya Baba, Sheikh Saad Bu, and Sheikh Ma al Aynin controlled different parts of Mauritania. These three influential men were marabouts, important Islamic religious leaders.

Sheikh Ma al Aynin was supported by Morocco; he in turn supported Morocco's claims to Mauritania. Following the death of Coppolani in 1905, the French were forced into battles against the Moors in the Adrar region of Mauritania. It would take another decade before Adrar was conquered. The Moors lost many of their precious cattle and camels in these battles and tried to get them back by raiding other nomadic Moorish encampments. By 1934 the last of these raids, and the French opposition to them, came to an end, and the French took over all of Mauritania.

COLONIAL POLICY OF THE FRENCH

Unlike other colonial nations such as England, Portugal, and Spain, France had its own ideas about how to control the people of French colonies. Also different was their attitude toward the value of those colonies. The most important element for the French in having colonies was simply that they had them. This notion made them feel that they had an empire. In order to rule the people in the colonies without spending much time or money on them, the French created a policy of cultural assimilation. This meant that the people they ruled would learn to live according to French culture, and abandon their own. They introduced the French language, French manners, and French food.

The French government decided in 1895 to group together seven of its territories in West Africa under one governing body, the Afrique Occidentale Française (AOF), which means French West Africa. The other territories were Côte d'Ivoire (Ivory Coast), Senegal, and Niger as well as areas known then as Dahomey, French Guinea, and French Sudan (which became Mali). The group was ruled from Dakar, Senegal. The French set up a bureaucracy with a European at the head. He, in turn, used local inhabitants to help collect taxes and carry out whatever projects the bureaucrats planned. They worked through the African chiefs who already enjoyed positions of authority in their villages.

TURMOIL IN FRANCE

When World War II began in 1939 in Europe, the French used conscripts from Mauritania and their other African colonies to fight for France. A year later, the Germans conquered France and imposed their policy of racial discrimination. The local Mauritanian chiefs, who helped govern their own people, were now forced to carry out these racist policies. When the war ended and the French regained control of their colonies, it was clear that the Africans in the army had made a large contribution to their victory. At the Brazzaville Conference, in the country of Congo, the colonies were given more freedom to rule themselves. They were intended, nonetheless, to remain under the control of France. In 1946 a new French constitution determined that the colonies were to be considered part of France itself, and the people living in the colonies were thus now "French."

The French were not interested in giving up control of their territories. They made sure that only a small number of Mauritanians were eligible to vote by setting very high standards. Only in 1956 was voting universal for all adults. There was little political activity in Mauritania after World War II and almost no movement for their independence from France. Other parts of French West Africa were much more active in demanding greater control over their own territories, and those actions paved the way for Mauritania's independence, too.

Though only a small percent of the people were aware of the political changes taking place, there were strong differences of opinion among them about the kind of government they should have. The dominant split was between the Arabs and the Berbers, who preferred an alliance with Morocco, and the black Africans who felt closer to the people in Senegal and Mali. Moktar Ould Daddah, the only native lawyer in Mauritania at that time, was named to head a council of ministers who worked under the direction of a colonial officer to construct a compromise. By 1957, Mauritania had its own government, led by Daddah, and a target date for independence, November 28, 1960.

What the country did not have was a city that could serve as the seat of government. The decision was made to create a new capital in Nouakchott on the land where an old fortified village, called a ksar, once stood. This was a clever political move. Nouakchott was located midway between the black farmers of the Senegal River Valley and the Moors of Adrar. Daddah now had to knit together the many different racial and cultural factions living in Mauritania. The vast territory was divided roughly into settled black Africans in the south and nomadic Arabs in the north.

Mauritania's first president Moktar Ould Daddah led the country for 18 years since its independence in 1961.

INDEPENDENCE BRINGS NEW PROBLEMS

Although the country was now independent, the conflicting factions persisted. The Moors dominated all the institutions of Mauritania, causing resentment among the black Africans in the south of the country. They particularly opposed the use of Hassaniya Arabic as the language of instruction in secondary schools. This virtually guaranteed that the black Africans would be kept from jobs and power in government.

Political parties began to form. At a time when the new nation needed all its people to create a sense of national unity, some of the different ethnic groups had very separate goals and allegiances. One group in the north wanted to unite with Morocco, while others wanted to join with Mali. Morocco offered a safe haven to the group because it supported Morocco's prior claim to all of Mauritania. Supporters of the union with Morocco created huge problems for the fledging country. Daddah, although well educated, had received his education in France and did not have close political or emotional ties to the people who had lived in Mauritania throughout the colonial period. He was considered to be too close to the French.

A NEW CONSTITUTION

As Mauritania was going through its own birth, France, the colonial power, was having a similar rebirth. A new government, known as the French Fifth Republic, wrote a new French constitution. This applied as well to the people of Mauritania, who were now considered part of the "French community." But Mauritania did not want to be part of the old France, it wanted to be part of the new Africa. Other African nations, including its neighbors in West Africa, were clamoring for independence.

Instead of remaining part of France, the people of Mauritania proclaimed themselves to be the Islamic Republic of Mauritania in October 1958 and created a new constitution. Just producing a document, of course, does not guarantee that everyone will accept the new rules. The tribal chiefs wanted to hold on to their positions of power. At the same time, the nomads who were the majority of the population were not good candidates for bureaucratic positions. Daddah worked hard to bring the very different ethnic and cultural groups together in the new country. By 1960 independence was achieved, and by 1961 the country had chosen to be ruled by one political party, the Parti du Peuple Mauritanien PPM, in English, the Mauritanian People's Party. The government was mixed, ethnically, with 10 blacks and 20 Moors named to the National Assembly. While this worked to unite the people, having a single party made it very difficult for people opposed to the government to organize and work for change.

Unrest, strikes, and demonstrations took place, especially over language issues. In 1966 the ruling government made it compulsory to study Hassaniya Arabic in secondary schools. It went a step further in 1968, making the language an official language, along with French. Underground, unofficial, and illegal political parties began to form, seeking more political freedom.

Then the country was hit by an extremely severe drought that lasted from 1969 to 1974. The drought devastated the nomadic population, killing their livestock and forcing them toward the cities, where they set up shantytowns. During this period, the urban population exploded from 8 percent of the total population to 25 percent. The government could not provide housing, services, or above all, employment for all these new city dwellers. Soon, the nomads' lives were turned upside down.

ECONOMIC AND POLITICAL UPHEAVAL

The young government then began to take a look at its position in regard to France, its former colonial master. One of the boldest changes was to create its own currency. Mauritania had been part of the West Africa Monetary Union which was tied to the French franc. In fact, many other former French colonies in West Africa still share a common currency, the CFA franc. Mauritania, instead, introduced the ouguiya.

In 1974 it took over control of the iron-mining company MIFERMA and named it SNIM (Société Nationale Industrielle et Minière, which means National Company for Mines and Industry), the iron mine that produced 80 percent of the country's exports.

Events outside Mauritania were proving to be equally difficult to manage. In 1975, the Western Sahara, which forms all of Mauritania's western border as well as part of its northern border, was going through its own political turmoil. The territory, known as the Spanish Sahara, had been claimed by Spain, which occupied it from 1884. The local people, known as Sahrawi, struggled against Spanish rule. The situation changed greatly there, however, when vast deposits of phosphate were found at a place called Bu Craa. Now, everyone wanted to control the territory.

On November 6, 1975, in a dramatic and bold gesture, the king of Morocco instructed his people to prepare to walk into the Western Sahara. It was called the Green March—green for the color of Islam. An estimated 350,000 Moroccans marched to the tiny city of Tarfaya in southern Morocco and simply walked into the Western Sahara. Spain saw that it was up against a formidable opponent, and in 1976 it turned its claim over to Morocco and Mauritania, jointly.

For Mauritania, the territory, now renamed Western Sahara, was a welcome barrier between itself and Morocco. It feared Morocco, which had claimed Mauritania in the past. It had good reason to be concerned. Morocco was far more powerful than Mauritania, and it had already said it intended to occupy the entire Western Sahara. By 1976 Mauritanian troops found themselves fighting Polisario Front guerrillas, a force of

Sahwari natives who found support in neighboring Algeria. The Polisario wanted to form the new government of Western Sahara.

The war was very costly for Mauritania. The country spent money it did not have to fund the war and suffered personal loss by the death of many Mauritanian soldiers. In spite of its small population, the armed forces rapidly increased from 3,000 to about 15,000 by 1978. In 1977 defense spending amounted to 60 percent of the national budget. The Mauritanians were upset at being taxed to pay for a very unpopular war. And the war was not confined to the Western Sahara. Nouakchott itself came under rocket attack. Other Arab countries, mainly Saudi Arabia, provided more money to continue the fight than Mauritania spent on

The Polisario Front forces in Algeria. Mauritania suffered greatly as a result of the war.

every other need of its people. This war drained the country's resources and undermined the government of Daddah.

In 1978, in an effort to bring an end to the war, Daddah named Colonel Mustapha Ould Salek as army commander. The commander repaid the favor in an unexpected way: he and a group of junior officers threw Daddah and the rest of his government out of office. They took over Mauritania and created a new government, calling itself Comité Militaire de Redressement National (CMRN), which means, Military Committee for National Recovery.

Salek proved just as unable as Daddah to solve the problem of Western Sahara. Within a single year his government was overthrown by another military group. Colonel Mhamed Khouna Haidalla emerged as prime minister and Colonel Mohamed Louly became president. Political maneuvering continued until July 1979 when Mauritania gave up all claims over the Western Sahara.

PRESIDENT TAYA'S RULE

In 1984, with the economy still struggling, Prime Minister Haidalla was overthrown and another military man, Colonel Maaouya Sid'Ahmed Ould Taya stepped into power. He proved to be a very strong ruler but one who favored his own ethnic group of white Moors over the black Africans and black Moors. He worked to restructure the economy and tried to improve agriculture and fishing. At the same time, though, he was notorious in his treatment of anyone who voiced opposition to his ideas, jailing people who made any moves against him.

Mauritania's Islamic law governed all civil matters other than those arising in modern institutions that could not have been foreseen in the religion, such as litigation involving automobiles and corporations. But it did cover criminal matters such as theft and murder. Under this law, a person is not presumed innocent. Because the government was poorly financed, suspects did not get speedy trials but, instead, were detained for long periods of time.

President Taya took an unusual step when he named three women to cabinet-level posts. They presided over mines and industries, the presidential cabinet, and the ministry of health and social affairs.

By 1987 desertification had pushed aside all of Taya's other problems. It claimed more than 90 percent of the land that was arable when the country became independent. The people of Mauritania now had to fight over the country's scarce resources, and that included jobs and

Former president of Mauritania, Maaouya Ould Sid Ahmed Taya.

education as well as good land. More than 80 percent of the country's nomadic herders moved into cities, forcing these open-air desert dwellers into a city life.

A border dispute in 1989 between farmers from Senegal and herders from Mauritania grew until it turned into violent rioting, looting, and the deaths of hundreds of people. In response, Mauritania expelled an estimated 100,000 people, while Senegal did the same thing. This created huge disruptions to both local economies.

When President Taya was reelected in 1997, the main opposition parties refused to take part in the elections. They did not believe there could be free and fair elections under his government. One opposition party, Action for Change, which campaigned for greater civil rights for the black Africans and for the descendants of slaves, was banned.

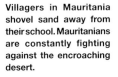

Villagers in Mauritania shovel sand away from their school. Mauritanians are constantly fighting against the encroaching desert.

Present Taya was reelected once again in 2003. That election was widely seen as fraudulent, and a series of attempts to overthrow the government took place in 2004.

In addition to desertification, the country suffered another natural catastrophe, in 2004, when locusts descended on Mauritania, wiping out the entire food crop. The country has now become dependent on food aid.

On August 3, 2005, a group calling itself the Military Council for Justice and Democracy seized power in Mauritania, ending two decades of dictatorial rule. It promised to return the country to democratic rule, and it kept its promise. A new constitution was approved, and legislative elections were held in 2006. Women won 17 seats in the National Assembly, and the elections were regarded as free and fair.

DEMOCRACY ARRIVES

In March 2007 the country held elections that were seen as a new start for the democratic process. Under the election guidelines, if no one candidate wins more than 50 percent of the vote, a second round of voting takes place in which the two top candidates compete again. Since there were 19 candidates running, it was unlikely that any of them would get 50 percent of the vote. The top two contenders each received nearly a quarter of the votes and faced off in the second round. Sidi Ould Cheikh Abdallahi beat Ahmed Ould Daddah to become Mauritania's first democratically elected president since independence in 1960.

One of the new leader's preelection promises was to finally put an end to slavery by punishing those who continued to hold slaves. He also stated that former slaves and their descendants would be given special consideration to try to make up for all the years they had suffered deprivation.

In November 2007, the United States established a new military command mission in Dakar, Senegal, just to the south of Mauritania. America's presence there began with the arrival of the Navy Cruiser USS *Fort McHenry*. It was intended to protect Mauritania and the other countries of West Africa against the worldwide threat of terrorism. The threat became very real the day before Christmas, 2007 when a family of four French tourists was attacked and killed while enjoying a picnic near the town of Aleg. The suspects were linked to a training camp run by terror group Al Qaeda, in neighboring Algeria. The attack was shocking because Mauritania has long been considered a very safe country and has been trying to develop its tourism industry.

Right: **Opposition member, Ahmed Ould Daddah, the half-brother of Moktar Oud Daddah, votes during the 2007 elections.**

Opposite: **Spain's Carlos Sainz on his way to winning the twelveth stage of the 29th Dakar Rally in 2007.**

Two weeks later (January 4), authorities cancelled the Dakar Rally (due to start January 5, 2008). This famous road race begins in Lisbon, Portugal and runs through parts of North Africa. In 2008, the racers were scheduled to spend eight days in Mauritania. The cancellation came after threats were made against the organization. The directors also acknowledged that the attack on the French tourists made it clear that these threats were very real.

The loss of the money brought in by the race, as well as the fear it has created in Mauritania, was seen as a great setback to Mauritania's recent moves toward democracy and unifying its Arab, Berber, and black African populations.

Mauritania enjoyed democratic rule for just one year. The newly elected president, Sidi Ould Cheikh, tried to show he was truly in charge by firing the top military leaders. The military leaders were furious at this loss of power. On August 6, 2008, they arrested Mauritania's president and prime minister and put an end to the country's brief period of democratic rule. The military leaders announced they would hold new elections "soon," and even said President Sidi Ould Cheikh would be allowed to take part in those elections.

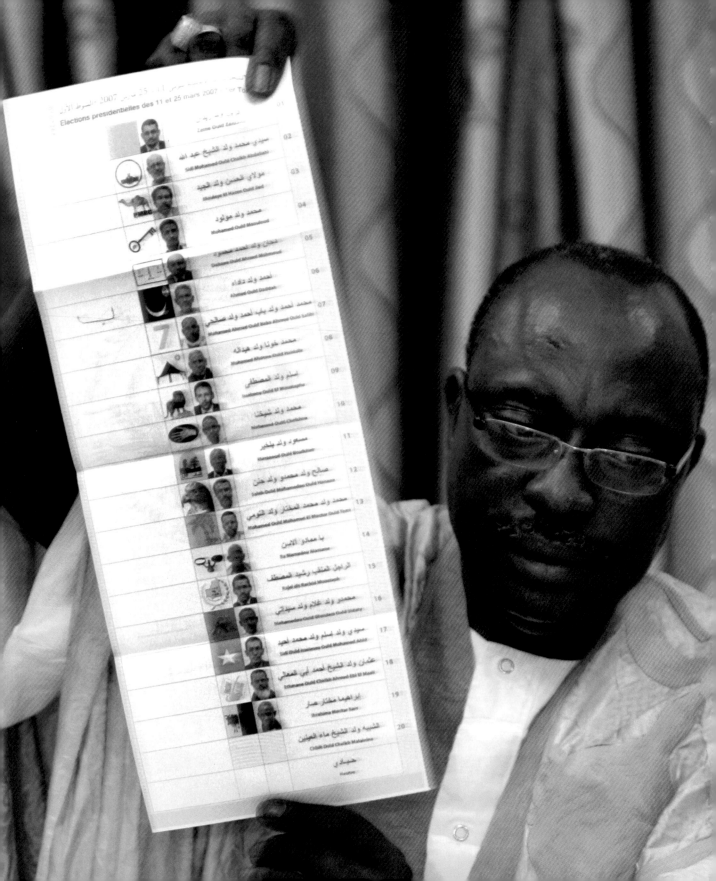

GOVERNMENT

SIDI OULD CHEIKH ABDALLAHI, the first president to be elected in a truly democratic process since the country became independent in 1960, was overthrown on August 6, 2008, one year after he was elected president. The military proved it was afraid of a genuinely democratic government. The election had been seen as truly free and fair. More than one million voters took part, voting at 2,400 polling stations. Three hundred observers made sure the process was fair. Sadly, it was not enough. The president and the prime minister were thrown out by the army although the military leaders promised new elections.

Mauritania's election process takes place in two stages. In the first stage, or round, all the candidates who want to run for the office of president appear on the ballot. If no candidate receives more than 50 percent of

Opposite: **The president of the Nouakchott polling center holds up a ballot before commencing the tallying of votes in 2007.**

Below: **Supporters of Mauritania's former president Sidi Mohamed Ould Cheikh Abdallahi at an election rally in 2003.**

PRESIDENT ABDALLAHI

Sidi Ould Cheikh Abdallahi was born in 1938 in the small town of Aleg, in southern Mauritania. He received his elementary education at a French school in neighboring Dakar, Senegal, and later studied economics in Grenoble, France. At that time there was no university or college in Mauritania. He has had a long history in government service. He served as Minister of State for National Economy, Minister of Water and Energy, and Minister of Fishing and Maritime Economy. He has also had experience outside Mauritania. For nearly two decades, he was a consultant with the Kuwait Fund for Arab Economic Development.

the total vote in the first round, the two candidates with the highest vote totals compete head to head in a second round. This makes the election extremely democratic because it gives all the candidates an equal chance to run for office. This system is based on that used in France, Mauritania's former colonial power.

In the first round of Mauritania's 2007 presidential election, no one received more than 50 percent of the vote, so a second round of voting was held. In the second round, Sidi Mohamed Ould Cheikh Abdallahi was elected president. He won with 52.85 percent of the votes. His opponent, Ahmed Ould Dadd, received 47.15 percent of the votes. President Abdallahi was inaugurated on April 19, 2007.

The president is also the head of state. The constitution allows him to serve two consecutive five-year terms. The first term of Mr. Abdallahi will end in April 2012. The head of government is the prime minister. He is appointed to this position by the president. President Abdallahi appointed Zeine ould Zeidane as prime minister, Zeidane took office on April 20, 2007.

Mauritania's official name is the Islamic Republic of Mauritania. The government is located in the capital, Nouakchott, and the country is governed through 12 administration regions, plus Nouakchott. The regions are Adrar, Assaba, Brakna, Dahhlet Nouadhibou, Gorgol, Guidimaka, Hodh Ech Chargui, Hodh El Gharbi, Inchiri, Tagant, Tiris Zemmour, and Trarza.

COMMUNITY COUNCILS

In 1992 Mauritania introduced a system that made the country more democratic and at the same time decentralized decision making. Villages elect their own mayors and councils, which govern them on local matters.

PRIME MINISTER ZEIDANE

Zeine ould Zeidane was born in Tamchekett in 1966, six years after Mauritania gained its independence. He was educated in Nouakchott before attending the University of Nice, in France, to study economics. He brings a strong background in banking to his position. He served as economic counsel to Mauritania's previous president, Maaouya Ould Sid'Ahmed Taya, at the World Bank. In 2004 he became governor of the Central Bank of Mauritania. He ran against Abdallahi for president in 2007 and came in third, receiving 15 percent of the votes. Zeidane then gave his support to Abdallahi in the second round of voting. President Abdallahi awarded him the position of prime minister in his new government.

One of the hallmarks of these councils is the open discussions they hold on any subject that affects daily life. When they were considering, for example, if a new national park should be created, some members of the council that oversees the delta region were strongly opposed to the park. Discussions dragged on, with the most educated people commanding the biggest say. But it turned out that the most educated people were the teachers, who had lost their connection with the natural environment. Because they had moved away to attend secondary school and then went to Nouakchott for teacher training, they were skeptical of the plans that were proposed. It was the people who remained behind, who were not educated but had a genuine understanding of the ecology of the region who saw the merits of the new plan.

THE NATIONAL FLAG

Mauritania's flag is green with a yellow five-pointed star positioned above a yellow crescent that lies with its pointed ends up, like a smile. The three elements of the flag: the crescent, the star, and the color green are all traditional emblems of Islam, but the way they are arranged on their flag is unique to Mauritania.

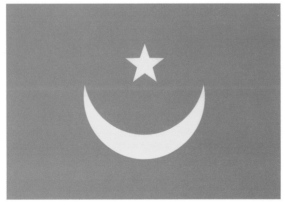

BRANCHES OF THE GOVERNMENT

The government has three branches: executive, legislative, and judicial. The executive branch is headed by the president and prime minister with a Council of Ministers.

The legislative branch has two houses, the Senate and the National Assembly. The Senate, called Majlis al-Shuyukh, has 56 seats. The members are elected by municipal leaders and serve six-year terms. Every two years a portion of those seats are up for election. This provides that the Senate will have experienced members as well as new members to evaluate and enact laws.

The members of the National Assembly, called the Majlis al-Watani, are elected directly by popular vote and serve five-year terms. The next

Female members of the Assembly of Democratic Forces attend a campaign meeting. Their political party was one of many running for elections in 2006.

Senate election will be held in 2009; the next National Assembly election will be held in 2011.

The political party that had the most votes in the last election in both the Senate and the National Assembly is Al-Mithaq, a coalition of independents together with political parties that were associated with the previous administration. Other political parties include the Alternative, or El-Badil; Centrist Reformists; Coalition for Forces for Democratic Change; the Democratic and Social Republican Party; and many, many more.

The Judicial branch consists of a Supreme Court, a Court of Appeals, and lower courts. The country is governed both by Islamic (Muslim) law, known as Sharia, and French civil law.

NATIONAL HOLIDAYS

Mauritania observes both Western and Islamic New Year's days. The Western New Year is always on January 1. The Islamic New Year varies according to the Islamic calendar, which is lunar. The country also celebrates Mouloud, the Prophet Muhammad's birthday. This date also varies according to the Islamic calendar. Mauritania observes May 1, Labor Day, which is celebrated by many countries around the world. May 25 is African Liberation Day and is the anniversary of the founding of the Organization of African Unity. July 10 is Armed Forces' Day. Mauritania celebrates the Muslim festival of Korité, marking the end of Ramadan, as well as Tabaski, another important Muslim holiday. The dates of these two events vary according to the Islamic calendar. On November 28, Mauritania celebrates its independence from France in 1960.

ECONOMY

MAURITANIA'S ECONOMY HAS NOT BEEN able to catch up with its rapidly growing population. The extreme climate and the encroachment of the desert limit the development of agriculture. These factors also discourage foreign companies from investing money in industries there. Mauritania also lacks the highly skilled and well-educated workers that might attract outside investors. Mauritanians have remained dependent on food aid, especially during times of drought. The World Food Program, supported by the United States and many other countries, delivers millions of dollars worth of food to the people each year. In 2007 the country produced less than 25 percent of the grain crops it needed. The rest had to be donated. Dozens of agencies and humanitarian groups around the world contribute money, food, and health services to the people of Mauritania.

The country's currency is called the ouguiya and is used only in Mauritania. The rate of exchange is about 270 ouguiya to one U.S. dollar (2007). Mauritania is considered to be one of the poorest countries in the world with some one-quarter of its total economy provided by contributions from international aid agencies.

Mauritania has very high taxes and duties on imported goods, some are as high as 45 percent. These import taxes discourage people from investing in the country.

Above: **The Mauritanian Bank for Trade and Industry.**

Opposite: A former nomad learns how to farm.

51

Opposite: **Men digging salt out of layers of clay.**

Although Mauritania's climate makes it almost completely unsuitable for normal agricultural activities and it has almost no farmland, half of its people still depend on agriculture, fishing, and cattle breeding.

The local economy is supported mainly by the mining industry, which is under the direction of the Ministry of Mines and Industry.

MINING IN MAURITANIA

Iron ore has been the country's main export product and has sustained the economy for decades. With the development of its gold, oil, and other mineral resources, the country has the potential of increasing its earnings.

The SNIM iron mine (Société Nationale Industrielle et Miniere) at Fderik-Zouerate and Guelb has been operating since 1963 in the northwestern part of the country and has been the main resource of the country. There, huge earth-moving machines dig into the ground and bring up ore, which is then processed by crushing. The ore is loaded into open railway cars that look like enormous buckets. The ore is taken to the port at Nouadhibou, where it is transferred onto ships.

Iron contributes half of all the export income of the country. Work is underway to upgrade and expand production through a major new drilling program. This very old mine needs serious upgrading to enable it to continue producing iron ore. One of the most important considerations in expanding work at the site is the amount of water that may be available for the processing work.

Mauritania also has significant reserves of copper and gold and recently began mining both of these metals. They occur in the same area, at Guelb Moghrein. Mining began after the government of Mauritania signed an agreement in 2004 with a Canadian company, First Quantum. The government owns 20 percent of the mine. The Moghrein Mine has an estimated 22.6 million tons of copper, while the Tasiast Mine has an estimated 30 tons of gold.

Gold is much more valuable than copper, and Mauritania is estimated to have 1,185,000 ounces of gold buried deep within the earth. The gold deposits are found north and east of Nouakchott. At the end of 2007, gold was selling for $725 an ounce. The cost to produce each ounce was then only $220 per ounce, so the profit potential is great. Small-scale mining began in 2005 and is expected to increase considerably, reaching 105,000 ounces of gold annually. In addition to the value of the minerals, these mining operations also provide employment to local people.

In addition, the country has tremendous reserves of phosphates, estimated at 160 million tons. Phosphates are vital fertilizers and used in the agricultural industry. Moreover, Mauritania has gypsum, sulfur, and salt—all important elements. Gypsum reserves are enormous. When mining began in 1973, the reserves equaled one billion tons. Much of the material that was mined was exported to neighboring Senegal, where it was processed in cement

factories, as Mauritania did not have any factories that could process the ore. Salt resources amount to 120 million tons and are recovered in two areas, Trarza and Tiris.

DISCOVERY OF OIL

Perhaps the most exciting news about mining in Mauritania was the discovery of oil and gas deposits in 2001 in the Chinguetti oil field in the coastal basin, offshore in the Atlantic Ocean. Oil production began in February 2006 and has improved the overall economy of the country dramatically. The Chinguetti oil field is located about 50 miles (80 km) west of the coastline and is worked by a group under the control of the Mauritanian government. The reservoir of oil in the field is located deep beneath the ocean floor. It is estimated that there are 120 million barrels worth of oil in the reserve, but it is not easy to reach. The cost to develop the resource is estimated at $500 million.

In order to reach the oil, the company has created a floating production, storage, and offloading system. Oil is pumped up from the seabed into platforms that float in the ocean. The platforms produce and store the oil, which is then transferred to storage areas until it can be loaded onto tankers. A huge special tanker, which can store up to 1.6 million barrels of oil, was also developed to hold and transport the oil.

FISHING

The waters off the Atlantic coast of Mauritania were among the richest fishing areas in the world. Estimates of the catch vary greatly, but all indicators pointed in one direction: by the 1980s, the waters were being overfished. That means that fish were being taken from the water faster than the fish could reproduce and replenish the supply. Foreign operators were taking an unknown amount of fish, trolling from large boats. The Mauritanian government did not have any way to patrol its own waters, so these poachers were able to continue plundering the waters.

TRANSPORTATION

Paved roads are very scarce in Mauritania. The harsh environment, lack of places to buy gas, and the concentration of people in the two main cities, makes travel by vehicle both difficult and, often, dangerous. The

Fishermen preparing to leave to fish. Many fishermen are beginning to find it difficult to make their living due to overfishing in Mauritanian waters.

lone train that runs between Nouadhibou and Zouerate is one of the most uncomfortable ways to travel in the world, but it is considered better, and safer, than driving across the Sahara.

The construction of the Trans-Mauritanian road between Nouakchott and Nema, in the southern part of the country, demonstrates just how challenging it is to build and maintain a road in Mauritania. Construction of the 685-mile (1,102-km) long road began in 1975 and was opened officially in 1978. It is known as La Route de l'Espoir, which means road of hope in French. This is the main paved road in the country and serves as a vital artery for transporting goods. There are also plans to include Mauritania in the Trans-Sahara Road, designed to link the country with the port of Lagos, Nigeria, in the south. This ambitious project has been under construction since 2001. The usual problems have slowed progress, especially the relentless sand that sweeps across the roadway. The extreme temperatures of hot and cold in the desert region cause the road surface to expand and contract, requiring constant and expensive repairs of resulting cracks.

The remaining network of roads includes a paved road that runs along the shore, connecting Mauritania's two main cities, Nouakchott and Nouadhibou. The road is dangerous to use because it is poorly maintained and it would be almost impossible to get help in the case of a breakdown. Paved roads also connect Nouakchott with Rosso in the south, Nema in the southeast, and Akjoujt in the north. The rest of the roads in Mauritania are sand tracks. They are difficult to use in both the normal dry season and after the rainy season.

It is hoped that, some day, the Trans-Saharan Road will be completed and will extend all the way through Morocco, giving Mauritania access to ports on the Mediterranean Sea, enhancing the movement of goods and visitors.

THE TRAIN IN THE DESERT

There is no official passenger train service in all of Mauritania, but there is a train that carries iron ore from the SNIM mine at Zouerat to the coastal port of Nouadhibou. This is the longest and heaviest train in the world when it is loaded with ore. It takes about 17 hours for the 220-car train which measures 1.5 miles (2.4 km) long, to make the trip. When the train leaves Nouadhibou, all the ore cars are empty and passengers jump on to sit in the open cars. It is broiling hot during the day and freezing cold at night, but it is the only form of public transportation in the region. Those who can afford to pay $4 can try to find a spot in the one passenger car attached to the train. Almost all people wind up sitting on the floor. Most people take the train only as far as Choum, a desert town about 12 hours traveling time from Nouadhibou. For anyone who works in Zouerat, the train is the only way to get to the coast.

People load everything imaginable onto the train, including goats and sheep, furniture, and bags of animal feed. They must load these goods on the train quickly because it only lingers in the station for fifteen minutes.

ENVIRONMENT

THE NATURAL ENVIRONMENT IS AT the heart of every aspect of life in Mauritania. With the Sahara forming most of its territory, the country faces a constant lack of water and arable land. Every year the Sahara moves southward, claiming 4 miles (6.4 km) of land. Nouakchott, the capital, was once in the Sahelian Zone. Now sand dunes have piled all around it. Drought and climate change have created some of this drying up of the land, but there are other, human, causes as well. Intensive farming causes the soil to lose nutrients. Overgrazing livestock on land until there is nothing left to hold the soil in place also adds to the drying up of the already vanishing land. The loss of farmland and droughts have forced people off the land and into Nouakchott.

Some programs are trying to help. The United Nations Development Program (UNDP), working with the H2O Africa Foundation, is tackling the problem of securing drinkable water for a group of families living

Left: **Cattle in rural Mauritania. Overgrazing by cattle have sped up the process of desertification.**

Opposite: **Erosion from strong winds have left strange formations like these in the deserts of Mauritania.**

in the village of Néré Walo. This village has three wells, which it uses during the wet season. When the wells go dry in the dry season, however, villagers must use the water from the distant Senegal River for drinking and for cooking. The project set up a tower to store water, along with two fountains to dispense water. By making water available where the people live, the women of the community, who traditionally carry water in very heavy buckets and containers on their heads, now have only a short distance to walk to get water for their families. Hauling water has never been seen as men's work.

Another group, the Community Water Initiative (CWI), has developed eight projects in Mauritania to improve access to clean drinking water. CWI works closely with people in their communities, giving small grants of just $20,000–$30,000 to create projects that are appropriate for the environment and the local culture. In Boghé, for example,

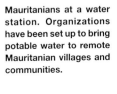

Mauritanians at a water station. Organizations have been set up to bring potable water to remote Mauritanian villages and communities.

they constructed a project where ceramic pots used for drinking water could be made by hand and sold by local people. Other water-related projects were carried out in Dar El Barka, Bababé, Magtar Lahjar, Timzine, and Towei Dieri.

Having a supply of safe water that is close at hand can better the lives of the people living in these small villages. Children are healthier, women are less likely to die in childbirth, and women do not have to spend so many hours a day walking to and from a water source.

THE SENEGAL RIVER

In 2004 a $10 million, four-year-long project began to improve the Senegal River Valley and provide better water and other resources

A RACE FOR WATER

In 2006 a team of three distance runners set out to highlight the need for water by embarking on an incredibly difficult journey: they chose to run across the Sahara from Senegal, running 4,850 miles (7,805 km) all the way to Egypt. A major portion of the run was through Mauritania. They ran the astonishing equivalent of two marathons a day every day, for 111 days. The three men, from the United States, Canada, and Taiwan, undertook the exhausting trip to show the hazards of living in the Sahara in a dramatic way, one that would grab the world's attention. They visited water-related sites in each country, including a dam under construction in Mauritania. The United Nations Development Program oversaw the project, which was captured in a documentary film, *Running the Sahara*. The film was produced by Academy Award–winning actor Matt Damon, who joined with the H20 Africa Foundation to help raise funds and awareness of the scarcity of clean drinking water in Africa.

for the human population as well as the wildlife that depends on this river. The Senegal River is the second longest river in West Africa, running about 1,118 miles (1,800 km) from Guinea, where it rises, and then flows west through Mali before it forms the border between Mauritania and Senegal.

The presence of the river itself is an attraction to people in the region. Through the years, more and more people have migrated to the river valley, putting more and more demands on the river. People there raise livestock, fish in the river, and draw its water to grow crops. On the Mauritanian side of the Senegal River, the Diawling wetlands are an important site, helping to support migratory birds, including sandpipers and flamingos. These birds fly in from distant places in Europe when

The Senegal River is an important resource in Mauritania and many essential activities like fishing and other daily chores are carried out there.

the weather there turns cold. They spend the winter months around the wetlands area before returning to Europe in the spring.

The building of two dams, in Mali, and the Maka-Diama dam on the Mauritania-Senegal border, near the Atlantic Ocean, put a huge strain on the river. A dam traps water that should flow down river. River water becomes sluggish and contaminated because its normal movement has been reduced. The oxygen levels fall, causing fish to die. In addition, drawing water for irrigation as well as for hydroelectric energy has changed the flow of the river.

In the past, the river had natural changes, responding to seasonal wet and dry conditions. This kept nature in balance, with each species adjusting to the changing environment. The region had a variety of plants that depended on each other for their survival. When the dams were built, they caused vast changes to this natural system. With a water level and a current remaining constant certain unwelcomed plants, especially weeds, as well as water-borne diseases, were able to thrive.

The current project aims to improve the management of the river so that it is once more a dependable and sustainable lifeline for the people of the Senegal River Valley. With the changes in the climate, however, the amount of water in the river is less dependable than in the past. Even with the best management, there may not be enough water to meet all the demands placed on the river. Both the World Bank and the UNDP are working with a local authority, the Organization for the Development of the Senegal River (Organisation pour la Mise en Valeur du Fleuve Sénégal), which was founded in 1972, to make the best use of this vital resource.

Three West African nations, Mali, Mauritania, and Senegal, jointly formed the organization because they all depend on the Senegal River.

Their goal is to manage the river in such a way that it will help increase food production, create income for local people, and help protect and preserve the natural environment.

In September 2007 unexpected torrential rains poured down over Africa in a huge area stretching right across the continent. Millions of people were affected, including those in Mauritania. Cooperative for Assistance and Relief Everywhere (CARE) set out to assist people with food, medicine, and water purification tablets in an effort to ward off diseases. In this desert country, too much water is as great a problem as too little. The land is unable to soak up the water, so it floods communities, washing out buildings and totally destroying the remaining farmland.

When the floods subsided, Mauritania returned to its fight against the encroaching desert. It is working to create greenbelts around Nouakchott and the area of Magta Lahjar, well south of the capital. The greening project at Magta Lahjar has been very successful at protecting a small section of roadway from the ever blowing sand.

SOIL DEPLETION

Sub-Saharan Africa, a region that includes all the nations of Africa that are located south of the Sahara, suffers greatly from the loss of usable soil. According to Kofi Annan, who is from Ghana and served as secretary general of the United Nations, a Green Revolution is needed to help provide Africans with enough food. One of the causes of malnutrition in Africa, he says, is that "almost three-quarters of Africa's land area is being farmed without the use of adequate fertilizer and improved seeds, and our soils are among the most depleted in the world." In Mauritania, where farming can be carried out in only a narrow strip along the Senegal River, the depletion of the soil is a major threat to food production.

OIL POLLUTION

The recent discovery of offshore Atlantic Ocean oil deposits near the Arguin Bank, regrettably, means that this delicate environment is greatly threatened. Accidental seabed pollution, the result of leaks, is of great concern. Perhaps even more significant, the oil drilling platforms sit right in the area where the Imraguen people fish. The platforms disrupt the natural rhythm of the fish and interfere with their feeding areas.

OASES

Mauritania's traditional economy included life around the oases. In old Hollywood movies, the stereotypical oasis was a magical place filled with palm trees, camels, and busy people going about their daily lives. That is not far from the truth. An oasis is a site with a natural source of

Date palms growing around the oasis in the Adrar desert.

water, deep in the ground. This water allows date palm trees to grow. The palms protect smaller vegetation planted in their shade, including wheat, barley, sorghum, and vegetables. This vegetation is then available for both human consumption and for small livestock that supply a family with meat and milk. Caravans have counted on these precious water sources for centuries.

NATIONAL PARKS

In a country that is primarily desert, the only national parks are located at the seacoast. The main reserve is Banc d'Arguin (Arguin Reef). The park was created in 1976 and named a World Heritage site by the United Nations Educational, Scientific, and Cultural Organization (UNESCO) in 1989. It is a natural wetland that runs for more than 736 miles (1,185 km) along the Atlantic coastline. Banc d'Arguin National Park is mainly an underwater reserve that features seals, large dolphins, marine tortoises, and crabs. Some land mammals are found in the region, too, including jackals and gazelles. Sand dunes line the edge of the land portion of the park. Between the water and the dunes visitors may find many

FISHING IN THE PARK

The Imraguen are fishermen who use traditional methods to fish for mullet and courbines. Overfishing, in part by the Imraguen but mainly by large-scale foreign fishing vessels, has depleted the quantity of fish in these waters. This has also led to a decreased number of seals, which depend on the fish for its food. The Imraguen are known for using dolphins as their fishing partners by getting them to herd fish toward the nets.

local plants, including the acacias gommier, a type of fig tree. The park itself includes an amazing variety of terrains, among which are sand dunes, coastal swamps, small islands, and shallow coastal waters. It is this variety of different types of environments, especially the sharp contrast between the desert and the water areas that has created an area of such importance. Migrating birds arrive from distant lands to the north to spend the winter in this rich environment. Dolphins that frequent these waters play a unique role in the lives of the fishermen. The dolphins herd fish into tight schools and then drive them into shallow water so the fishermen can catch them. The fishermen wait with their nets and scoop up some of the fish that the dolphins have gathered.

At Banc d'Arguin the most numerous migrating birds are sandpipers. Visitors may see the birds from small boats, only with the permission of the park service and with a guide accompanying them. They are not allowed to approach the birds, even by boat, during the two mating seasons each year.

Migratory birds are so important to the world's environment, that in 2006 UNESCO designated April 9 as World Migratory Bird Day. Birds are the world's greatest navigators. They may start their journey to Mauritania from thousands of miles away, in Europe, where they breed and raise their young. The young birds have just a few months to grow and learn to fly. As soon as the weather in Europe begins to turn colder and the days grow shorter, it is off to the south. Young birds learn

The coast along Banc d'arguin.

the route from their parents, flying in with huge numbers of their kind who make the annual flight to warmer days. Millions of birds in all make this tremendous trip each year. Some spend the winter at Banc d'Arguin, while others use it as a resting place before heading even farther south. The instinct to migrate is so strong, the birds return to the exact same places year after year. For that reason, it is vital that not one single park or wetland be abused or lost.

DIAWLING NATIONAL PARK

Mauritania's other national park, Diawling National Park, was established in 1991. It also lies along the coast. Diawling is located on the Senegal River and covers a former floodplain. The existence of the park was very controversial since it meant relocating—against their will—people who lived in the area. The same thing had happened 20 years earlier on the Senegal side of the river, where another national park was created. The people living in villages on the Mauritanian side of the river had close tribal and family ties with the people on the Senegal side of the river. They knew that they were going to be forced from their homes just as their Senegalese relatives had been. They also were to be prevented from using this rich land for grazing and fishing. The government of Mauritania, however, felt that the park would help many more people by conserving the entire delta and by developing uses of the park that would not overburden the delicate environment.

After a great deal of community discussion, the government appointed representatives from the three villages that were closest to the park to be part of the management team. Elders were signed up as honorary guards. They became part of a team that worked to educate others about the value of conservation.

The Diawling National Park is being conserved mainly for the benefit of the local population. The environment is extremely fragile and is not suited for traditional tourism.

For most visitors, Mauritania offers a chance to see vast expanses of desert and to visit the ancient cities where great Islamic libraries were created. Travel is generally limited to four-wheel drive vehicles, and to those with knowledgeable guides. Most people travel to Mauritania to experience firsthand the extremes of nature. They are the kinds of visitors who enjoy roughing it and do not expect to find typical tourist facilities, such as Western-style restaurants and hotels.

A group of tourists sitting under the shade of the acacia tree. Visitors to Mauritania experience and see desert life firsthand.

CLIMATE CHANGE

For Mauritania, global climate change has been a very real and very local phenomenon, one that affects daily life throughout the country. While most of the country's weather-related problems come from the relentless advances of the Sahara, recently it has had to deal with exactly the opposite problem: too much water. In 2006 and 2007 rainfall across the middle of the African continent washed out dozens of villages and roads and left 1.5 million people without farms, crops, livestock, homes—bereft of any way to support themselves.

MAURITANIANS

THE VAST TERRITORY OF Mauritania has a population of just 3,270,065 (est. July 2007).

The population is very young, with scarcely any people over the age of 65. In 2007 there were only about 42,867 women and 28,564 men who were 65 years of age or older. Life expectancy is just 53.51 years with women living an average four years longer than men. The country has a very high birth rate. Each woman has an average of nearly six children.

Mauritania is often described as a bridge between the Arabic north and the black African south of the African continent. In reality, the nation has a number of ethnic groups that remain very separate from one another. Class, or social ranking, is very important in Mauritania. The country has

Left: **Two young Peul girls. The Peul are considered to be part of the Black African group.**

Opposite: **A Mauritanian man carries his child.**

two main ethnic groups that may be described as black Africans and Arab-Berbers. Within the black African group are the Haalpulaar, which includes the Fulfulde, Peul and Fulani, and the Soninke. There are also a small number of Wolof people who live in the south. Most of the Wolof live in neighboring Senegal, across the Senegal River. An even smaller number of Bambara people live in Mauritania, as the majority live in neighboring Mali.

SOCIAL STRUCTURE

Mauritania's rigid social order developed early in its history. The different groups of people who came into the territory eventually established a social structure in which one group dominated another. It began in the 17th century when the Berbers were defeated by the nomadic Arabic Bani Hassan. The Berbers then served the Arabs. Black Africans were at the bottom of all these social groups, and in time became unpaid laborers, virtually as slaves. Although these groups were socially separate, they spoke the same language, Hassaniya Arabic. They became known as Maures, Maurs, or Moors. The name of the country came from this word. Mauritania is the land of the Moors. Other black Africans, culturally related to the black Moors, were free and lived separately in the Senegal River Basin.

There are also a group of black Moors called Haratin. Throughout much of Mauritania's modern history, the Haratins were taken as slaves and forced to serve the white Moors.

The Haratin actually outnumber any of the other groups in Mauritania. It is estimated that about 40–45 percent of the population is Haratin, black Africans make up about 30 percent, and the white Arab-Berbers or white Moors account for about 25 percent.

SLAVERY

In the long history of Mauritania, there are people who lived free and others who were slaves. But unlike West Africans who were abducted from their homelands, put on ships, and sent to foreign and distant lands to work on plantations, in Mauritania an entire race of people was taken into domestic slavery. They toiled as unpaid labor in the homes and fields of the upper classes, the white Moors. The black Moors, known as Haratins, have been kept in slavery for centuries.

No one needed to put chains on them, since they had no place to run away to. They did not even know there was another way to live. Kept totally uneducated, unable to read, write, or even count to five, they were barely fed and never earned any money. After 500 years, an entire slave

Despite slavery being formally abolished, there are still black African slaves in Mauritania.

class had been shaped to exist only to serve the people who enslaved them.

In the north, where the Arab-Berbers are dominant, upper-class women were not supposed to perform any physical work. Instead, slave women performed all the household work. This is one reason it has been so difficult to eliminate domestic slavery. It has become such an accepted part of this culture that many Arab-Berbers still believe it is their right to have slaves.

After Mauritania became an independent nation in 1960, the government attempted to abolish domestic slavery by enacting a law against it. That law had very little effect because it was not really enforced. The government of 1980 enacted yet another law against slavery, but that law was not enforced either. Slavery continued to exist throughout the rest of the 20th century, even though national spokesmen insisted that it did not. It did not disappear simply because it had been outlawed.

In 1997 it was estimated that Mauritania still had 90,000 slaves. Born into slavery, they were passed along as property. As one girl said, "God created me to be a slave just as he created a camel to be a camel."

There is no future in her mind because she does not even know how to think about the future. The never-ending present is just a round of work: fetching water, making meals, cleaning house, looking after animals.

Families that keep slaves in Mauritania are so convinced that they have a right to own these people, that they fight against the government when by law it frees these people. One said he would have to be paid for the loss of "property" when his slaves were taken from him, because he did not recognize any law that said it was illegal to keep slaves.

Since so many rural Mauritanians lost their livestock because of the drought and flocked into the cities, they have had much less use for slaves. They feel no obligation to take care of those who have waited on them hand and foot. They simply abandon them and leave them without food. These "freed" slaves often have even less of a life than they had before. They do not even have a corner of a room to sleep in.

On August 9, 2007, Mauritania's parliament made the practice of slavery illegal and a criminal offense. Anyone keeping a slave could be sent to jail for ten years. The law also spells out the actual conditions of slavery, which include forced marriage. Although some people feel the law is weak, it is a huge advance for Mauritania. It will take a long time for the practice of domestic slavery to disappear, however, since the number of people still held as slaves is so large.

MOOR SOCIETY

The Moors, also spelled Maurs or Maures, who give the country its name, are divided into white Moors and black Moors. The white Moors, also called Bidan, are a mixture of Arabs and Berbers, while the black Moors, also called Haratin, are a mixture of Arabs, Berbers, and Negroid or black Africans. People identify themselves as being Arab or African. Both the

Opposite: **A family living within the El-Mina quarters, which is mainly inhabited by the descendants of slaves.**

75

white and black Moors identify themselves as Arab, but only the black Arabs identify themselves as African, too.

Within Moorish society, people achieve social status through their heritage and race and also through their occupation. Among the most prominent of these are skilled craftsmen known as artisans and storytellers. The artisans provide all the items needed in everyday life and include blacksmiths, jewelers, woodworkers, leatherworkers, potters, weavers, and tailors. Almost all of these crafts are reserved for men. Women are permitted to do weaving and tailoring.

Entertainers, poets, and musicians occupy their own special place in society. These lively arts are highly valued, and those who practice them may have patrons among the noble families. Among those considered to be on the lowest level of society are fishermen, salt miners, and nomadic hunters. Two groups that are very important to Moorish society are the warriors known as *hassani* and the religious leaders, called *zawaya*.

It is almost impossible for people to move out of their social levels in Mauritania. A person born into any one of these groups is likely to remain there for life. Individuals in these groups, including the entertainers and the artisans, tend to marry within their own group and, in this way, continue their separate paths through life.

Black Moors were forced into slavery early in Mauritania's history, and they have remained a slave class ever since. White Moors treated their slaves as property, selling or moving them to other families as they chose. The black Maures carried out all household chores as well as the farmwork. Among the Moors, the most important relationships are those of the extended family. A group of males who are related to each other, along with their wives, sons, and unmarried daughters, is considered the extended family. Marriages take place within the same clan, and marriage between first cousins is preferred. This is against the practice of most parts of the world where marriage between first cousins is not allowed for fear of inbreeding.

Most of the black Africans in Mauritania belong to the Toucouleur clan, which is a subgroup of the Fulbe. The Toucouleur, also known as the Halpularen, can be identified mainly by their dialect. They speak Fulfulde, a dialect of Pulaar. These languages are closely related.

In addition to these two ethnic groups, the other black African people in Mauritania are the Soninke and very small numbers of Wolof and Bambara. The Soninke are also part of a much larger group of people who live in a vast stretch of west Africa including Mali, Burkina Faso, and Côte d'Ivoire. They are found mainly around the Senegal River.

The Fulbe are known by several names and are spread throughout the Sahara and Sahel regions of north Africa. In Senegal they are called Peul, while in Nigeria they are known as Fulani.

Within their own societies, the black Africans are divided into three social classes: on the top rung are the nobles; there is a middle class of people below them; and at the bottom is the servant class.

IMRAGUEN

The Imraguen are an ancient people who live on the Atlantic shore. They have been fishing in the waters near Banc d'Arguin throughout the history of the land of Mauritania. The word Imraguen means "those who gather life," because they pull living creatures from the sea. As far back as the 15th century, Portuguese explorers recorded the presence of the Imraguen and their traditional sailing boats. Their unique quality is the way they work with wild dolphins to find fish and herd them into nets.

LIFESTYLE

UNTIL THE DROUGHTS OF THE 1970s and 1980s, most Mauritanians were nomadic. They lived in tents, moving from place to place when they needed to find grazing for their livestock. They accumulated very few material possessions, but they did treasure the items they used in everyday life. Nomads are very hospitable, sharing whatever they have. Life in the Sahel—the zone near Senegal—and the Sahara is very harsh. People depend on one another for their survival there.

When the droughts made it impossible to keep livestock and nomadic people were forced into the cities, especially into Nouakchott, they had to adapt their customs to city life. Many of the people who flocked to Nouakchott, however, brought their tents with them and set them up at the edge of the city, which continues to grow every day. The tents give them a place to live, but the huge numbers of people have very little space for their families. People are forced to live very closely together,

Opposite: **A motorbike passes a donkey and cart on the streets of Nouadhibou. The old and the modern often exist side-by-side in Mauritania.**

Left: **A group of nomads sit in the shade provided by a tent.**

and this sets up a situation where diseases can spread quickly. Crime is also on the rise, since so few people have jobs and they no longer have livestock to supply them with food.

RURAL LIVING

In the rural areas, people live in tents. A tent houses one family, which includes the parents and the children. The tent provides shelter from the harsh climate. It has large flaps that allow air to pass through but that can be closed during sandstorms. Rugs are placed on the ground, and people sit or lounge on them. Families place their tents in groups called encampments. At the center may be found the tent of the chief who rules this group.

Nomads live in tents like this. The rural landscape of Mauritania is dotted with such dwellings.

Traditionally, girls who lived in rural areas learned homemaking skills—how to take care of children and how to run a household—from their mothers. Some attended religious schools, where they were taught to read verses from the Koran, but literacy was not considered important or even useful for a girl. The things a girl needed to know could be learned at home. Boys acquired the skills they needed from their fathers and other male relatives. They especially learned how to take care of livestock, the family's most important possession.

Fathers were responsible for seeing that their daughters were prepared to make good marriages. They accomplished this by making the girls as attractive as possible, and this meant seeing to it that they weighed a lot. They arranged marriages for their daughters. These arrangements were often made when the girls were still children, so that by the time the girls were teenagers, their futures were secure through marriage.

People living a truly nomadic life would pack up their tents every six months or so to find new grazing ground. But those who were settled took care of their farms, where they grew food crops and raised their families in permanent settings.

URBAN LIVING

Because of the changing climate, the rapid movement of Mauritanians into Nouakchott has pushed many people into a new way of living. The special skills they learned as nomads have no place in the city. Women, however, take their weaving skills with them and make mats that can be sold in the markets. Men look for work as unskilled laborers. Those who are literate try to get jobs in the government.

People in urban and rural areas alike eat together, taking food from a large bowl. It is customary to serve small glasses of green tea with sugar and mint. Serving tea is a large part of Mauritanian hospitality, and drinking tea is also a way to pass the time.

TACKLING TRASH

With the huge increase in the population of Nouakchott, garbage has become a major problem. When people lived as nomads, they had little trash because they had few possessions. As soon as they move into the cities, however, the amount of garbage increases. They now use foods and other products that create waste. In the past, they simply threw this waste out on the streets and alleys. When trash, especially food waste, is allowed to sit in the sun, it quickly becomes a breeding ground for disease.

In 2007 Nouakchott started a major effort to gain control of this problem with a campaign called "A Clean City for Everyone," directed by the Urban Community of Nouakchott. A weapon in the fight against disease, the program includes uniformed sweepers who clean the streets.

TRADTIONAL DRESS

Most Mauritanian women and men wear traditional clothes. For black African men and women, the customary garment is the *boubou*. If he can afford it, a man will wear a richly embroidered, very loose-fitting, sleevleless robelike garment that reaches all the way to the ground. It has deep vents on the sides. Underneath it, the man wears loose trousers called *seroual*, usually made in white, blue, or black, and a roomy long-sleeved shirt, usually in the same color. The garments may also be made of much plainer and less expensive material. The women's *boubou* is usually a loose-fitting single garment with very wide sleeves that she can push up and drape over her shoulders while she works. It may have a wide, open

Muslim women usually wear traditional dress, but do not cover their faces.

neckline, allowing her to put it on easily. If she can afford it, her *boubou* will be elaborately embroidered, too. It will always have a matching scarf, tied into an intricate headdress. Traditionally, Muslim women cover their heads. Moorish women wear a *malahfa*, a long garment wrapped around the body. They also cover their heads.

In the desert, men and women wrap their heads entirely to protect themselves from the sun and the blowing sand. Men wrap their heads in a very long length of fabric, creating a headdress called a *chèche*. When the wind begins to blow, the *chèche* can be drawn up around the mouth for further protection. During the worst sandstorms, the very tail end of the *chèche* may be pulled up around the eyes.

Among black African women, another piece of fabric, called a *pagne*, may be wrapped around the waist and draped into a long skirt. This is combined with a *boubou* as well as a head scarf.

Wearing many layers of fabric in such a hot climate is actually the best way to deal with the heat and the sun. The loose layers allow air to circulate, creating a kind of natural air conditioning, while the multiple layers protect the skin from the harmful rays of the sun.

Local villagers from Chinguetti wearing traditional *boubous* and drawing water from a well for travellers.

MIGRANTS

Their search for a better life is at the heart of one of the most difficult problems facing Mauritanians today. Although the population is quite small, the number of available jobs is even smaller. Opportunities are very few, and young men, in particular, need to find a way to make money. Without money they cannot afford to get married. A man who is not married does not merit a proper place in Mauritanian society. This compels more and more black African men into leaving the country. They embark on a very dangerous journey, hoping to travel over the Atlantic Ocean to the Canary Islands. These small islands are part of Spain. Once a person reaches the Canary Islands, he has in fact arrived in Europe.

Arrested illegal immigrants awaiting repatriation are held at a police station in Nouadhibou. Many Africans try to migrate to neighboring Spain in a search for a job.

For some black African Mauritanian families, sending a boy off to make his way to Europe is a kind of "rite of passage," a way to prove himself in the world. An entire family will pool whatever money they have to fund his trip out of Africa to a new life in Spain. There the pay is many times what he might earn at home—if he can find a job.

The sorrow is that so many never make it that far. They pay human smugglers for a place on all kinds of flimsy boats, setting out on the rough waters of the Atlantic Ocean. Almost every week, Spanish news reports tell of immigrants whose boats have capsized somewhere between the West African coast and the Canary Islands, nearly 1,000 miles (1,609 km) away. The overloaded boats rarely have any kind of safety features, such as life rafts or life preservers. The immigrants usually do not know how to swim. For most, this dangerous trip is the first time they have been near the ocean.

The nations they are trying to reach have tried to discourage them from even setting out. They send out coastal patrols in an effort to turn back the ships before they reach shore. As a result, professional captains, commanding large, safe ships, have abandoned the smuggling business. It is too risky for them because if caught, they could lose their ships. The business then falls to those who are willing to risk everything, including their passengers' lives, to make money. These boats are rarely suitable to make the trip. Often the boats run out of fuel and the men are left to drown in the ocean. They rarely have enough food or drink for those on board. Sometimes boats are so crowded that there is hardly any room to sit. Some are just rubber rafts, not at all suitable for the journey. It is estimated that thousands, most from other West African nations, have perished in the effort to reach this foreign land. Thousands of others are caught before they reach shore.

For those who survive this awful journey, however, their troubles are far from over. The Canary Islands are mainly a tourist destination, and they do not have jobs for the huge number of migrants who managed to wash up on their shores. In 2007 more than 31,000 actually made it to the islands. These migrants do not have skills or much education. All they have to offer is their labor, and there are just too many of them.

At the same time, the migrants, who are considered to be illegal because they do not have valid travel documents, do not want to be sent home. So they throw away anything that would identify where they came from. The government of the Canary Islands cannot send them back, since it does not know where they came from, so they are sent to Spain. There the men and boys disappear into the streets of the cities and try to find work. If they speak French, many try to go to France, where they feel they might have a better chance at finding work.

WORKING ABROAD

Other Mauritanian men do find work abroad, but they do it in a much safer way. They get visas to travel legally. For this group, most of them Wolof people who also live in neighboring Senegal, the destination is New York. There you can see them on street corners, selling handbags, sunglasses, scarves, and hats. They spend their days with merchandise set up on tables, peddling to passersby returning at night to apartments they share with others like themselves. There is a vibrant West African community in New York City, clustered in a section of Harlem. They often return to Mauritania each year, carrying electronic goods that they sell. Then they return to New York to make money again on some of the city's most fashionable streets. You can hear them chatting to their friends in Wolof while they wait for customers.

Still others go to France, once known as the mother country. These black Africans are more permanent residents. They settle in African neighborhoods in Paris, including the section known as the Bastille, bringing in their families as soon as they can. Many of them also bring their Mauritanian customs, including having more than one wife. This pits them against French civil law, and it also creates extreme tension with French citizens. These large families, with two or three wives and many children, are a drain on the resources of the country. For the women, life in France is extremely difficult. Usually restricted to their apartments, they have little connection with the cosmopolitan city, and they do not have their own extended families to turn to.

It is not unusual for a Mauritanian man living in Paris to return home to marry another woman without his first wife knowing anything about it. Suddenly, he returns to Paris and simply says, "This is my new wife." Now they are expected to live together in the same apartment. But this is not like living in Mauritania where each wife has her own small house to live in with her children. In these crowded apartments, they must share what little space there is. This is a clash of cultures, one African, the other European. By continuing to live in such different circumstances from the rest of the French people, the Mauritanians guarantee that they will never be really integrated into France.

MARRIAGE

Most marriages in Mauritania are arranged, especially when it is the man's first marriage. It is very important to maintain a strong connection with one's own community, so marriages are usually between two people in the same local area. Often these marriages are between cousins. Marriage is seen as a way to strengthen the support and obligations within a community. People rely on each other to a much greater extent in rural areas. There, where living conditions are harsh, it is important to have such a support system. In many ways, marriage provides a kind of welfare system that the government of Mauritania does not offer. By building up its larger community, the married couple can look for help from an extended family group.

For women, marriage is necessary but it is also a very difficult road. In reality, women in these marriages do most of the hard work looking after livestock as well as the household. These practices are very rare in big cities, but common in villages. Very few Mauritanian women work for cash income outside the home. Marriage offers financial support that is vital. In village life, when a woman marries, she moves to the household of her husband's family. She immediately must establish relationships with the other women of this family. She is seen as another pair of hands to do household work, but also as another mouth to feed. In cities, a woman goes to her husband's house.

In the Muslim religion, women are not considered to be equal with men. In court, for example, it takes the testimony of two women to equal that of one man. Under Sharia, the Muslim system of law, a woman may inherit only half the share that her brothers receive.

POLYGAMY

In the Muslim religion, Islam, a man is permitted to have more than one wife at the same time, provided he treats his wives equally. But in practical, everyday life, it is not possible to treat two or more wives equally. When a man decides to take a second wife, he does not have to tell his first wife. He simply marries the second wife and then brings her home. The first wife is now referred to as the elder wife. The second wife is always younger, and the first wife sometimes treats her as a servant. For the man, it is considered prestigious to have more than one wife. It shows that he has enough wealth to support them.

OVERFEEDING WOMEN

Throughout Africa, finding enough food is usually a parent's biggest problem. In Mauritania, however, the problem is trying to convince parents not to overfeed their daughters. In traditional Mauritanian society, even among educated women, it is considered socially desirable to be overweight. Men prize brides who are overweight, although for men, it is the tradition to be thin.

In order to put pounds on their young daughters, parents force girls to drink up to five gallons of milk a day, either camel's milk, which is very rich in fat, or cow's milk. Only the very poorest people, who cannot afford the milk, stuff their girls with cream, butter, and couscous, virtually forcing her to eat more than she wants. A young woman who is very round and very heavy is considered worthy of being married.

While the unhealthy practice is now discouraged by the government, people out in the villages still practice this tradition. Most women weigh 200 pounds, a very heavy burden on their bodies. Some weigh as much as 300 pounds.

In 2003 the government began a campaign urging women to stop the practice of overfeeding their children. They created television and radio commercials to show how unhealthy this practice is. The health risks are understood now by the more educated people; however, most Mauritanians do not have televisions to watch. In a country where only half the adult women can read and write, tradition still plays the most important role in a woman's life.

FEMALE CIRCUMCISION

Mauritanians have traditionally insisted that their daughters undergo a painful and unnecessary surgery. Formerly known as female circumcision, but now more usually called female genital mutilation, the operation

Female circumcision is a dangerous practice that can cause many problems.

removes part of a girl's genital organ. In many Islamic countries, it is considered necessary to prepare a girl for marriage. Women are now protesting against this practice, however, which is usually performed by other women who have no medical training. It often causes lifelong problems, especially during childbirth.

Today, many more educated Muslim leaders understand that this practice is harmful, and they are working to bring it to an end. Their influential role is crucial in seeing that the law forbidding the practice is carried out.

EDUCATION

In 1999 Mauritania's educational system established Arabic as the only language for first-year students in primary school. French is added to

Mauritanian children in school.

the curriculum for second-year students. In addition, regional training centers were established, focusing on the economy of the specific region. This was intended to provide education that related to people's actual experiences. Secondary school education was increased to allow seven full years of courses. English was added to the curriculum in the first year of secondary school. Scientific courses, however, were to be taught only in French. This included math, science, and computer studies.

Mauritania has taken great strides in making education available for girls of primary school age. By 2005 girls slightly outnumbered

In Mauritania the literacy rate for girls has increased.

boys in primary schools. In spite of the government's best efforts, the quality of education is poor because the number of schools and teachers cannot keep up with Mauritania's high birth rate. Children get only a very basic education.

By the time students reach high school age, the number of girls who continue their education drops off sharply. Only about half the girls go on to secondary schools. The numbers drop even more at the higher education level. At the University of Nouakchott, the first school of higher learning in the nation, just 25 percent of the students are girls. This is still a great improvement over the past, and it is hoped that by the year 2015 the proportions will have evened out. In addition, there are two other schools, the Teachers' Training College (École Normale Superleune) and ENA (École Nationale d'administration).

Without a solid education, girls have far fewer choices. They need skills to get better jobs and also to make them able to understand the world they inhabit. Education relates to every aspect of their lives.

LITERACY

Since girls were rarely educated in the past, there is a low literacy rate in Mauritania among adults today. As adults, barely 50 percent of women can read and write. The percentage for men is not much better: about 66 percent of adult men can read and write Arabic. Being able to read is crucial to having a hand in the development of a nation. Literate people can read political documents and make better voting decisions. They can read directions on medicines and help safeguard their health and that of their children. They can also understand the laws that govern them. And women can better comprehend their rights, as women, as wives, and as citizens.

COMMUNICATIONS

Modern communications play a small role in the lives of most Mauritanians. As is typical of most African countries, there are fewer landline telephones than cell phones. These countries, including Mauritania, simply jumped over landline technology. By the time they were developed enough to be seeking telephone service, it was much more practical to turn to cell phones. Usage is restricted to just the major cities. In 2005 there were an estimated 745,600 cell phones and only 41,000 landlines in use. The country has Internet service as well as its own servers. An estimated 14,000 were Internet users in 2005.

Mauritania has two television broadcasting stations, Television of Mauritania and Channel 2, one AM radio station, and one FM radio station, all of them owned or controlled by the government. The radio stations broadcast in national languages as well as in French. There is one daily newspaper, *Ach-chaab*, one bi-weekly called *Journal Officiel* and a monthly publication, *Le Peuple*. All three are published in both Arabic and French.

HEALTH

Because Mauritania has such a high birth rate, nearly all rural women spend most of their time having children and taking care of them. Their own health suffers because there is so little medical care available in the country. Many women die during childbirth because they have not had any medical care at all during their pregnancies. Most women give birth without a doctor or a nurse in attendance. Many infants needlessly die shortly after being born. Some of them suffer from malnutrition because their mothers have not had proper food during their pregnancy. These mothers are often anemic, and cannot produce enough milk to feed their infants. For most infants, there is no other choice than mother's milk. Baby food and formula are not available and would be too expensive for most of the population. A lack of clean drinking water is also a major factor in people's poor health.

This poor start in life is one factor in the low life expectancy in Mauritania. A child born there today has a life expectancy of just 53 years. Harsh living conditions contribute to this low figure, too. Child labor is another factor. Mauritania's high birth rate of five to six children per woman leads to children being put to work at an early age to help feed themselves and their families. It is estimated that children make up 13 percent of the country's working population.

Women wait with their babies at a maternal care health clinic in Nouakchott.

DISEASES

A lack of health services makes it very difficult for diseases and other illnesses to be treated in their early stages. Even in the capital there is only one large hospital. Throughout the entire country, there are just 25 health centers, 15 of them devoted to maternity cases.

Unlike many African nations, Mauritania does not have a great number of people suffering from AIDS. In 2003 it was estimated that about 9,500 people were living with HIV/AIDS and that fewer than 500 people had died of the disease. Mauritania does have a very high risk of diseases resulting from dirty water and food, especially hepatitis A and B and cholera. People are also at risk of meningitis. In some regions, malaria and Rift Valley fever also occur.

TRACHOMA AND GUINEA WORM DISEASE

The people of Mauritania suffer from diseases that are typical of countries without enough clean water and poor health care. One of the most devastating, yet easily treated, diseases is trachoma. Trachoma is an infection that affects the eyelid, causing scarring. The scarring then scratches the cornea of the eye, leading to blindness. In some parts of Africa, the disease is endemic, which means it is present everywhere. Now the International Trachoma Initiative (ITT), a plan that intends to eliminate the disease worldwide by 2020, is in place. Mauritania has become the tenth country to launch a nationwide campaign to wipe out this dreadful disease, which affects

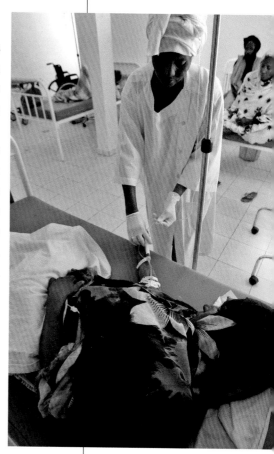

A nurse treating a patient with HIV.

84 million people in 55 countries. The ITT group is working to distribute an antibiotic that has been donated, entirely free of charge, by the drug manufacturer. The program began in Mauritania in 2004 with 140,000 people, most of them women and children, undergoing the treatment. Women are considered most at risk because they take care of the children who have the infection and they themselves become infected over and over again. Doctors working on the program expect to have eliminated the disease in Mauritania by 2020.

Mauritania has already solved another serious health problem, guinea worm disease, thanks to the effort of the Carter Center, the organization founded by former U.S. president Jimmy Carter and his wife, Rosalynn Carter. The Carter Center offered financial assistance as well as special cloth water filters to help rid Mauritania of the disease. Guinea worm is a parasite that affects a person's entire health. It is very painful and also saps a person's energy so that a victim is unable to carry out normal daily activities.

The parasite thrives in dirty drinking water, so it affects anyone who uses this water. In the case of Mauritania, to treat people in the remote parts of the country it is necessary to depend on camels, horses, and donkeys to carry the materials; to train local workers; and to keep accurate records. The Guinea Worm Eradication Program began in 1990 when Mauritania conducted a nationwide, village by village, search for cases. They found 8,301 cases in 511 villages. Treatment began in 1992. By 2004 the program was declared a complete success. There was not one case reported after that time. On November 15, 2006, President Carter presented an award to Mauritania, as well as to other African countries, for completely having stopped guinea worm transmission. This is a remarkable achievement.

MALARIA

Malaria continues to threaten the health of Mauritanians. This is a disease that is widespread throughout Africa. It is transmitted by mosquitoes, and once again, dirty water is a factor. Mosquitoes breed in still or stagnant water and then they fly from person to person in search of blood, carrying the infection with them. Malaria is found mainly in the southern part of the country, along the Senegal River, where there is a high concentration of the population.

Infants and children are especially hard hit by malaria because they have not yet developed immunities, but adults are also greatly affected by the disease. It weakens people and keeps them from working and taking care of their families. Malaria causes an extremely high fever alternating with chills. In Mauritania malaria affects so many people it is considered the number one public health problem. In 2003, 167,423 people were reported to be infected with the disease.

It has also been reported that mosquitoes are becoming resistant to chloroquin, the most common drug in use. Lack of clean drinking water and malnutrition also account for many deaths from malaria and other common diseases. What is more, the disease has now been reported in Nouakchott, the crowded capital city, for the first time.

In 2003 the Global Fund designated $824,125 for a two-year program to improve malaria prevention in Mauritania, including donating millions of bed nets. One of the most effective and least expensive ways to prevent the disease is the use of bed nets to keep the mosquitoes from biting children while they sleep.

Infants and children also suffer from diseases that can be controlled such as measles. While immunization programs are in place, they have not reached enough children.

RELIGION

MAURITANIA'S OFFICIAL NAME is the Islamic Republic of Mauritania. When it became independent in 1960, the country chose this name to proclaim that it identified itself entirely with the religion of Islam. Almost everyone in Mauritania is a Muslim, a follower of Islam. Islam is not just the official state religion, it also includes the laws, known as Sharia, that people must follow in their daily life. By defining itself as a Muslim country, the government hoped to unite the different ethnic and cultural groups that make up the population.

Mauritania is one of only three members of the Arab League, a group of Muslim countries that recognize the state of Israel. It does so, in part, to reflect its support for the United States.

The religion of Islam has two main branches, Sunni and Shi'a, also called Shiite. In Mauritania the majority of Muslims belong to the Sunni branch. This branch is then divided into four schools of laws. In Mauritania the particular type of law that is followed is called the Maliki rite.

Muslims are instructed in their religion through studying the Koran, also written as Qur'an, and a body of information called the sunna.

The religion began in the year 610 when Muhammad, a merchant from Mecca, a city in present-day Saudia Arabia, began to preach. He said that he had received divine messages from Allah, through the angel Gabriel, and he wanted to share these messages. His preaching set him against his fellow citizens because he declared that there was only one god. To

Above: **The Saudi mosque in Nouakchott**

Opposite: **A Koranic tablet found in the once-great city of Islamic learning, Chinguetti.**

escape the increasing hostility from the other peoples of Mecca, he fled to Medina. The flight itself is known as the hijra and is the moment when the birth of the religion is recognized.

After Muhammad died in 632, there was a disagreement about who his rightful successor should be. This led to a split, forming the two branches of Sunni and Shi'a Islam that exist to this day. Muhammad's followers gathered his words together into the Koran, the holy book of Islam. They believed that these words came directly from Allah. In addition, other teachings formed the hadith, which means "sayings." Finally, they recorded his way of behaving and created the sunna. These three elements are the guides to living a Muslim life.

A kiffa wood and mud mosque in the region of Assabra in Mauritania.

THE FIVE PILLARS OF FAITH

Muslims follow five basic tenets, or beliefs, which guide them every day. These duties are known as the Five Pillars of the Faith.

The first is the daily statement of faith that says, "There is no God but Allah and Muhammad is his Prophet." This was an important step of the belief in a single creator of life. Allah is an Arabic word that means "supreme being."

The second pillar is prayer itself. Muslims are instructed to pray five times a day, facing in the direction of Mecca. Men and women pray separately. They pray wherever they find themselves, although they try to go to a mosque, the Muslim house of prayer, when possible. Wherever they pray, they spread out a small prayer rug to kneel on.

The third pillar is to give zakat, or charity. This is an individual responsibility, but at one time it was an actual tax, placed on a person's wealth.

The fourth pillar, Ramadan, is a period of fasting, named for the ninth month of the Muslim calendar, which is based on the cycles of the moon. This means that the actual month in which Ramadan occurs changes slightly from year to year, eventually moving through all the seasons. During this month-long devout period, Muslims may not eat or drink anything during daylight hours. In the winter months, the number of daylight hours is briefer than in the summer months. Breaking the fast, in the evening, is a very joyous time.

The fifth pillar is called the hajj. The hajj is a journey to the holy city of Mecca that takes place during the twelfth month of the lunar calendar. Muslims are obliged to make this journey only once in a lifetime and only if they have the financial means and are healthy enough to do so. When a man has completed this journey, and has taken part in the special rites

Children study the Koran, which is in Arabic, using prayer boards. They learn about the Islamic way of life from a young age.

that are performed in Mecca during that time, he is known as a Haj. A woman is called a Hajjah. This is a title of great honor in Islam.

Islam also places a series of moral obligations on its followers. They are expected to be generous, fair, honest, and to show respect for others. They are not allowed to gamble or to charge excessive interest on loans. They may not eat pork or use alcohol. Every aspect of daily life is spelled out in the Sharia, the Islamic law.

Children learn the verses of the Koran by reciting them and by writing them on slates, over and over again. There are 114 chapters that must be memorized.

The government and the people believe that Islam helps to unify the country's people, whatever their ethnic background or caste. A cabinet-level Ministry of Culture and Islamic Orientation, as well as a High Council of Islam, was instituted to be sure that proposed legislation conforms to Islamic beliefs.

Although Mauritania proclaims Islam to be the religion of the country and its people, it does allow freedom of religion. There is a very small number of non-Muslims, who worship at Catholic churches in Nouakchott, Atar, Zouerate, Nouadhibou, and Rosso. Most of the Christians are French people who live and work in the country.

Through the Press Act, the Mauritanian government has made it illegal for non-Muslims to distribute materials promoting their religions. It is considered very dangerous for non-Muslims to try to convert Muslims to their beliefs. The government believes that this would undermine the unity of society. It is also illegal to use a mosque for political activity, including distributing material for any political cause.

CHINGUETTI

The desert town of Chinguetti is known as the seventh holy city of Islam. By the 13th century it was already known for its libraries, which were filled with hundreds of Islamic manuscripts. These are kept, preserved, and protected by local families. During the 17th and 18th centuries, it was an important religious and intellectual center that served as a stopover for pilgrims making the hajj to Mecca. The ever-shifting sand dunes have largely buried the city but some buildings still remain, including the mosque, which dates from the 13th century. For a time in the mid-1990s, severe floods uncovered parts of the settlement that were buried beneath the sands. When normal desert conditions returned, the sands swept in once again. Today the mosque in Chinguetti is on the World Monuments Watch List of the 100 Most Endangered Sites.

LANGUAGE

THE OFFICIAL LANGUAGE OF MAURITANIA is Hassaniya Arabic, a mixture of Arabic and Berber. It is spoken by white Moors and the Haratin, the black moors. It might seem unusual for these very different groups to share a language, but it makes sense when you remember that the Haratin were often slaves of the white Moors. People who live in the same house must be able to communicate with each other. Although the ethnic French population numbers only a few thousand, French is the language of business and government, a hold over from

Opposite: **A newspaper salesman along the street of Nouakchott.**

Below: **A historic manuscript at the city of Chinguetti.**

colonial days, and is widely spoken among the most educated part of the population. Mauritania also has national languages, including Peul, Wolof, and Soninke. These are spoken among those ethnic groups. Both Arabic and French are used in the school system. The government emphasizes education in Arabic but not in the other languages. This puts those who speak only one of the other languages at a great disadvantage. They are limited in the kinds of jobs they can find. Without a knowledge of Arabic, for example, Mauritanians are shut out of much of the life of the country.

SPEAKING ARABIC

The Arabic language unites people in North Africa and the Middle East. It also brings together all Muslims who learn to read the Koran, which was written in Arabic. The Arabic alphabet has 28 letters and is

COMMON ARABIC WORDS AND PHRASES

Arabic	English
Anna mush fahim.	I don't understand.
Shu hatha?	What is this?
Ismee	My name is
Bikam hatha?	How much is this?
Na,am, aiwa	Yes
La	No
Al salaam a' laykum/marhaba	Hello
Ma salaama	Good-bye

written in a flowing cursive script across the page, from right to left. It is the second most used alphabet in the world.

The literacy rate, the number of people over the age of 15 who can read and write is estimated to be just over half the population. In 2000, 59 percent of men and 43 percent of women were said to be able to read and write. This is a tremendous increase in the number from just a generation earlier.

GREETINGS

Whatever language people speak, they address each other with great courtesy. In the desert, especially, when people meet, they first inquire about each other's health. Then they ask about the other person's family members. Next, if the travelers are still nomads, they ask about the other person's livestock, which is the source of their wealth and their livelihood. No one would think of jumping into a specific topic without following this age-old ritual. These greetings are part of an oral tradition in which people share their knowledge in storytelling. Histories are memorized by repeating them over and over, by parents telling them to their children, by grandparents passing on their memories and knowledge.

With this kind of information, for instance, a nomad would know about water sources, called oases, that allow travelers to journey across the desert. Without this knowledge, travel would be impossible. Oases are maintained by specific families who live around them. When a traveler approaches an oasis, he must request permission to draw water from the well. This is a matter of life or death for both the oasis dweller and the visitor.

ARTS

MAURITANIA'S ARTISTIC AND CULTURAL heritage is ancient, and this history has been recognized by UNESCO. Four ancient cities, Ouadane and Chinguetti in the north and Tichit and Ouallata in the southeast, that were built as far back as the 12th and 13th centuries, have been designated World Heritage Sites. Among the treasures the organization intends to protect are ancient manuscripts, numbering about 33,000, that were long held in 800 mainly private libraries. These documents contain the nation's written cultural history.

The World Bank is helping to support the protection of the ancient manuscripts by providing special boxes that preserve the delicate materials. These towns were also designated as worthy of the World Heritage List

Opposite: **A Soninke woman uses her fingers to paint patterns on the wall of her house in Djajibinni, Mauritania.**

Below: **An Islamic text from the 16th century. The World Bank is trying to preserve these delicate artifacts.**

The ancient cities of Mauritania, like Chinguetti, are under constant threat from the encroaching desert sands.

because they are fine examples of traditional desert life. Carvans traveling from Chinguetti were a vital factor in the trans-Saharan trade route. As many as 30,000 camels could be assembled to make up a caravan. Today they are merely ruins that just hint at the complex life that was lived there seven centuries ago.

The World Bank has also established associations to support traditional handicrafts, including goldsmithing, silversmithing, carpet weaving, and the making of tents, and leather goods. Performing and literary arts, including musicians, poets and writers, are also helped. The two organizations that were created are the Mauritanian Association for Art and Culture and the Festival of Nomadic Music, which staged its first event in 2004.

According to Mauritanian writer Moussa Ould Ebnou, Ouadane was one of the most important centers of Islamic learning. There, libraries and madrasas (schools where the Koran was studied) contained thousands of manuscripts. At that time, manuscripts were used instead of bound books. Ouadane and the other ancient desert towns are threatened by the advancing sand that creeps in everywhere. In courtyards, the sand sweeps in relentlessly and piles up against the collapsing walls.

CULTURAL HERITAGE

Mauritania's oral tradition—storytelling that is passed along from one generation to the next—has now been captured on cassette tapes, a vital resource for the future. Mauritania has a rich artistic tradition with artists, writers, and musicians who continue to bring the country's varied cultures to life. In 2007 Culture and Communication Minister Ahmed Vall Ould Cheikh announced that prizes would be awarded annually to honor Mauritania's best poets. The awards will be given to poets who write in Arabic, Fulani, Wolof, and Soninke. Poet Cheikh Abou Chejja received the first Arabic poetry prize, while Mohamed Ould Taleb placed second.

FILM

One of the Africa's greatest filmmakers is Mauritanian-born Abderrahmane Sissako. His film *Bamako* captured many prizes, including the prestigious Cannes Film Festival award. He also made *Heremakono,* "Waiting for Happiness," which also won many awards. This film is set in Nouadhibou, where a 17-year-old boy named Abdallah finds himself unable to relate to the people or the life he sees around him. It emphasizes

Mauritanian director Abderrahmane Sissako at the International Cannes Film Festival.

his inability to speak the local language, showing how painfully isolated people can be within the same country. The film took a top prize at the 2002 Cannes Film Festival.

The dialogue employed both French and Hassanya Arabic languages.

HANDICRAFTS

In the National Museum in Nouakchott, visitors may view exhibits of prehistoric pottery and other ancient artifacts depicting Mauritania's Moorish history. The nomadic lifestyle, now almost vanished in Mauritania, is on view here through displays of camel saddles, cushions, boxes, floor covering for tents, and other household objects once prevalent in the desert.

Mauritanian handicrafts include every object made for use in the daily life of nomads. Beautifully decorated chests to store clothes, exquisite rugs made for use on the floors of tents, and silver tea sets are made by hand and treasured. These will become even more valuable, since the nomadic lifestyle has almost disappeared because of the droughts.

Traditional rug making continues and may be seen at one of the rug factories in Mauritania. There, girls and women weave wool into beautiful scenes. Classic Mauritanian rugs from Boutilimit are made of camel, goat, and sheep hair. Women also make hand-knotted carpets with the traditional motifs.

MUSIC

Mauritania's international singing star Aicha Bint Chigaly has appeared at music festivals around the world. She is a descendant of griots, storytellers who relate the history of their people, often while playing music. Aicha

Bint Chigaly sings in Arabic and accompanies herself on a four-stringed lute called the *tidinit* and also plays a wide, shallow drum. Women usually perform on the *ardin*, a 10–14-string harp lute.

The Moorish musicians are known as *iggawin*. They carry within themselves a venerable tradition of music that is learned and passed along through the generations. Dimi Mint Abba, another important Mauritanian performer, started to learn music when she was eight years old. Her mother taught her to dance and to play percussion instruments, including the *ardin* and the tambourine. Khalifa Ould Eide learned music from his father, playing the *tidinit*. His father was a great *tidinit* player, and Khalifa left school when he was twelve years old to study singing and pursue a music career.

A popular singer from Mauritania is Malourna Mint Moktar Ould Meidah.

LEISURE

PEOPLE OF ALL AGES IN Mauritania enjoy playing a board game called *golorgal*. This game is played throughout Africa and is variously called wari, aware, ayo, and mancala. It is called *kraur* in Hassaniya. It is played on a wooden board that is generally rectangular in shape. Two rows of six little cups are scooped out to form the playing surface. There is also a larger cup at each end of the board. The playing pieces may be pebbles, beads, or seeds, almost anything that can be moved easily. The aim of the game is to move these beads from cup to cup and acquire the beads of the opposing player.

In the desert, people do not even need a board. They just hollow out spaces in the sand to create a playing surface. There are plenty of little pebbles around to use as counters.

Play begins with one player distributing his seeds around the board in the cups. There follows a complicated series of movements in which players lose or acquire seeds until he or she has won all the pieces in the game. The game is played by people of all ages, although it takes a lot of skill to be able to see at a glance how many seeds are in each cup and how to proceed. The game moves very fast and provides hours of fun for the players.

There is little opportunity, however, for leisure activities in Mauritania. Most of the day is spent on getting the basic necessities of life: food and water. For many people, walking to a water source and then carrying the water back home is the most time-consuming task they perform. Food preparation takes up a large part of a woman's day. Children must be cared for. At family meals, people talk and share their day's experiences.

Mauritania has a strong oral tradition in which storytellers recite the history of the people and pose riddles and puzzles. They also recite poems.

Opposite: **A group of boys in Chinguetti play soccer on the street.**

115

This is how children learn about their culture and their ancestors. Children also spend a great deal of time memorizing sections of the Koran.

In some areas, women paint walls with geometric patterns. The Muslim tradition does not allow religious art that features human or animal life. Instead, Muslims use the beautiful letters of the Arabic alphabet, especially phrases from the Koran, as decoration as well as floral and geometric designs. These are used on all kinds of surfaces.

BALL GAMES

Mauritania is part of the International Rugby Union. Although its team is known more for losing than winning, it is part of the Rugby World Cup and is proud to take its place in this classic sport. In 2007 the World Cup was held in France.

Right: **The Mauritanian national rugby team pose for a squad photograph before their match against Senegal in 2004.**

Opposite: **Egyptian player Ahmad Fathy (*in red*) contests for the ball with Mauritania's Kamara Abd Al-Azez (*in yellow*) during the African Cup of Nations qualifier clash in 2007.**

Rugby is similar to American football in that it is played with an oval-shaped ball. The resemblance to American football ends there, however, as rugby players wear very little protective gear. The object of the game is to score with the ball rather than to hit the other players and try to knock them to the ground. Instead, the players try to outmaneuver each other by running around them and making quick, unexpected turns.

Mauritania also takes part in the African Cup of Nations, an event that pits national soccer teams against one another. In many parts of the world, soccer is referred to as football, but it should not be confused with American football. Soccer is played with a round ball, similar in size to a basketball. The players score goals by moving the ball around with their feet or bouncing it off their heads. They are not allowed to touch the ball with their hands, which makes soccer a very challenging game. It demands a great deal of mental agility as well as the ability to run hard and change course swiftly. Soccer is played by children using almost anything that they can find to make a "ball."

LAND YACHTING

The winds that sweep across the Sahara have created a most remarkable sport: land yachting. Instead of sailing on a body of water, these "yachts" fly across the Sahara, taking advantage of 50-mile per hour (80-km per hour) winds. The first land yacht race took place in 1967 when a group of intrepid adventurers crossed the Sahara. The vehicles set out from Algeria and then crossed a huge section of Mauritania, because the wind blows steadily, allowing the "sailors" to ride their odd vehicles across the desert. They entered Mauritania in the very northwest corner and then continued to the southwest, finally reaching Nouakchott. The Mauritania portion took three weeks! Since this is a race in the desert, competitors do not try to get too far ahead of each other. No one wants to be lost in the desert sands. That is a huge looming hazard because the winds that

An English yachtsman pushes his yacht as he competes in the Sahara Sand Sailing competition.

fill the sails also bring up swirling sand and dust. Someone can be racing right in front of you and be totally out of sight.

At some points in the journey, camels and their riders appear to challenge the yachts. While the yachts outrace the camels, they are torn apart by the rough terrain. The uneven ground and the pebbles that cover the surface grind through the tires, which must be replaced frequently. Each team goes through more than 100 tires before they reach Nouakchott. In order to cross the Sahara in Mauritania, the yachts pick up local guides who know the desert the way we know the streets in our own towns.

Mauritanians cheer on land yachts as they near the finish line.

FESTIVALS

MAURITANIA IS A VERY TRADITIONAL society in which the people prefer to celebrate special occasions with their families. The only national holidays are Independence Day, on November 28, and Constitution Day, on July 10. For those in the north, June and July mark Guetna, the season when dates from palm trees are gathered. This is a time when people gather from around the country to celebrate the harvest of this important desert fruit.

Harvesttime is a traditional season to celebrate and also a time when many people chose to marry. A successful harvest means there will be enough food to feed wedding guests.

The end of Ramadan and the return from a hajj are also times of celebrations. These are very festive occasions and center around food. If a family can afford it, the head of the family is expected to slaughter a large animal such as lamb. The animal is prepared and then shared with many family members. Naturally, in such a hot climate, the meat must be eaten quickly or it will spoil. The important times of life such as the birth of a child or a marriage ceremony are also occasions when an animal is offered. Sharing this special meal is also a way of reinforcing family relations. The family is at the heart of Mauritanian culture. Funerals are also important occasions for celebrating a person's life and for family reunions.

Other events that Mauritania celebrates are the National Festival of Folk Music and the Festival of Nomad Music.

DESERT ROAD RALLY

Every year since 1983 Mauritanians have been welcoming some of the most intrepid travelers in the world. These are participants in the Lisbon to Dakar Road Rally. Known as "The Dakar," this is a race that rewards

Opposite: **An aerial view of the Dakar Race Rally where more than 2,500 people and 900 vehicles gathered. The Dakar Race Rally is one of the most prominent festivals in Mauritania's calendar.**

endurance as well as navigation skills for racers from all over the world, competing on all kinds of vehicles, including cars, trucks, and bikes. Organizers work with their African counterparts who know the land and the challenges it presents.

The most challenging part of the race, by far, is the crossing of the Sahara. The route varies every year as does the distance. In 2007 the race covered 4,000 miles (6,400 km). (The 2008 race was cancelled due to threats against the organization.) Hundreds of competitive racers entered Mauritania at Zouerate, crossing over from Western Sahara. They raced their way to Atar, Nouakchott, Tichit, Kiffa, Tidjika, and Nema before heading south into Senegal. For Mauritanians who still live in the desert,

Spain's Nani Roma navigates his car during the tenth stage of the Dakar Road Rally.

it comes as no surprise that some competitors still lose their way in the shifting sands. While the racers have good communications, the desert remains a formidable obstacle. Even in the 21st century, crossing the Sahara is considered a tremendous challenge and a major achievement.

While the race brings financial gains to the countries it crosses, there are also benefits that come from showing lesser known countries to the rest of the world. While news from Africa is mostly grim, here the continent can be shown as an exciting and exotic place to visit. The local peoples come into contact with the foreign visitors, and together, they make a human connection. The value that the Dakar brings to the regions it crosses are not only financial. This top-tier sporting event, the largest rally in the global circuit, lends a powerful image to each country it visits. Dakar's media coverage links the countries to a prestigious event that provides an upbeat picture, far removed from the political turmoil, health care concerns, and drought typically making the headlines. The geographic and cultural insights generated by the rally give a concrete boost to Africa's image.

Mauritanian rider, Zidane Soued Ahmed Medis, takes a moment before embarking on the 15th and final stage of the Dakar Rally.

FOOD

IN TRADITIONAL MAURITANIAN CULTURE, food preparation and sharing food plays a very large role. In good times, when food is available, people find time to enjoy meals taken together. Unfortunately, Mauritania is not able to grow or produce all the food the country needs. It is very dependent on food aid from international organizations. Meals are always taken at home. In the traditional nomadic culture of Mauritania, people sit on the floor, on woven mats or animal hides, and share food from a large bowl. The bowl may be made from a calabash, a kind of gourd. A meal is often in the form of a stew that may be taken directly from the bowl, using one's right hand—the only hand that one is permitted to eat with in Arab cultures.

The stew is usually a mix of meat, generally lamb or goat, or sometimes it might be fish, mixed with millet (a grain), sweet potatoes, or couscous.

Left: **Couscous is sometimes incorporated into the Mauritanian diet.**

Opposite: **Women selling their wares and produce at the market.**

Fish balls or dried fish are served in areas where fish is available. Juices are served with the meal, and tea is served afterward.

In urban societies, where people have come into close contact with French cultural ways, other foods have been introduced into the diet, including the long thin loaves of French bread (baguettes) which is always found in former French colonies.

Special foods are prepared to mark important and festive occasions. A wealthy man is expected to slaughter an animal, usually lamb, to mark the end of Ramadan and also the annual return from the pilgrimage to Mecca, the hajj. Animals are also sacrificed to signify very important occasions, such as when a baby is named, at the conclusion of an initiation or circumcision ceremony, to celebrate a marriage, and to honor a funeral.

MAIN MEALS

The main daily meal is taken either at lunch or dinner, depending on the cultural or ethnic group. Among black Africans, the main meal is more often taken at noon. Among the Arab-Berber group, the main meal will usually be taken in the evening.

TEA CEREMONY

The tea ceremony is a much-loved tradition in the desert where the serving of three glasses of sweet green tea, flavored with mint, is the basis of hospitality. It is impolite to refuse the tea. Although it might seem odd to serve very hot tea in the hot climate, it has the effect of evening out the temperature of the air with the temperature of one's body, and it is very refreshing.

A nomadic family may have its own silver tea service, kept in the family for generations. It is used with great ceremonial flourish when offering tea in a tent. Visitors in the desert are so rare they are welcomed with tremendous hospitality. It is also a basic courtesy to share food and drink with someone who has traveled such a difficult route. Even those nomadic people who have been forced into Nouakchott and Nouadhibou because of the droughts, still serve tea in their tents.

FOOD AID

Every one of the natural disasters that have hit Mauritania, droughts, locusts, and floods, has destroyed much of the country's own food resources. Farmers have lost both their crops and their livestock. For years, Mauritania has depended on food aid from international agencies such as the United Nations World Food Program and World Vision.

In the drought years from 1983 to 1985, more than 60 percent of Mauritania's supply of grain came from food aid. Even in the better rain

Above: **Mauritanian hospitality is often shown by serving tea to guests.**

Opposite: **A boy carrying baguettes.**

127

years of the late 1980s, only about one-third of needed grain came from local production. Food aid provided another third, while government imports made up the rest. Mauritania has not been able to feed its own people for many years.

Extremes of weather have brought Mauritania either too much water or too little. In 2002 a bizarre rainstorm killed nearly 120,000 cattle, sheep, and goats. Normally, these animals would have allowed people to survive until their next crops came in. This was the start of multiyear period of intense drought. In 2003 a drought-relief program was working to supply at least 88,800 people who were at risk of starvation because of the loss of their crops, farmland, and livestock.

A woman with her pruchases at the main market. A severe drought in Mauritania translated into a shortage of food for thousands.

The World Food Program considered some of the regions in Mauritania to be the worst affected in Africa, in part because the country was so unknown to most of the world. The more visible and familiar droughts in East Africa claimed most of the attention, and most of the food aid. Neighboring countries in West Africa were suffering, too. People there had also used up their grain reserves and were skipping meals. Many children were dying from malnutrition.

At the end of 2006, a survey by UNICEF revealed that at least one quarter of all Mauritanian children under the age of five were suffering from chronic malnutrition. The World Food Program has increased its aid to Mauritania and is currently assisting 40,000 children there with food aid.

An aid worker loads food into a World Food Program truck. A large portion of Mauritania's food supply comes from food aid.

AFRICAN LAMB STEW

(The following two recipes are meant to be combined and eaten as a one-meal dish.)

2 pounds lamb, cut into small chunks
2–3 tablespoons olive oil
2 onions, chopped
3 garlic cloves, thinly sliced
3–4 turnips, peeled and chopped
1 cup pumpkin or winter squash, peeled and chopped
2 medium tomatoes, chopped

Brown the meat by stirring quickly in the hot oil in a large stewpot with a tight-fitting lid. Reduce the heat. Sauté the onions and garlic until golden. Add the rest of the vegetables, stirring for 2 to 3 minutes. Add water to cover, about 2 cups. Cover the pot and simmer until the vegetables are tender and meat is cooked.

Serve with couscous.

COUSCOUS

2 packages couscous (5 ½ ounces)
1 ¼ cups water
1 cup dates, pitted and chopped
½ cup raisins
8 ounces chickpeas, precooked
¼ cup butter or olive oil

Combine water and butter or olive oil. Bring to a boil. Stir in dry couscous. Remove from heat, with a fork. Mix the dates, raisins, and chickpeas into the fluffed couscous.

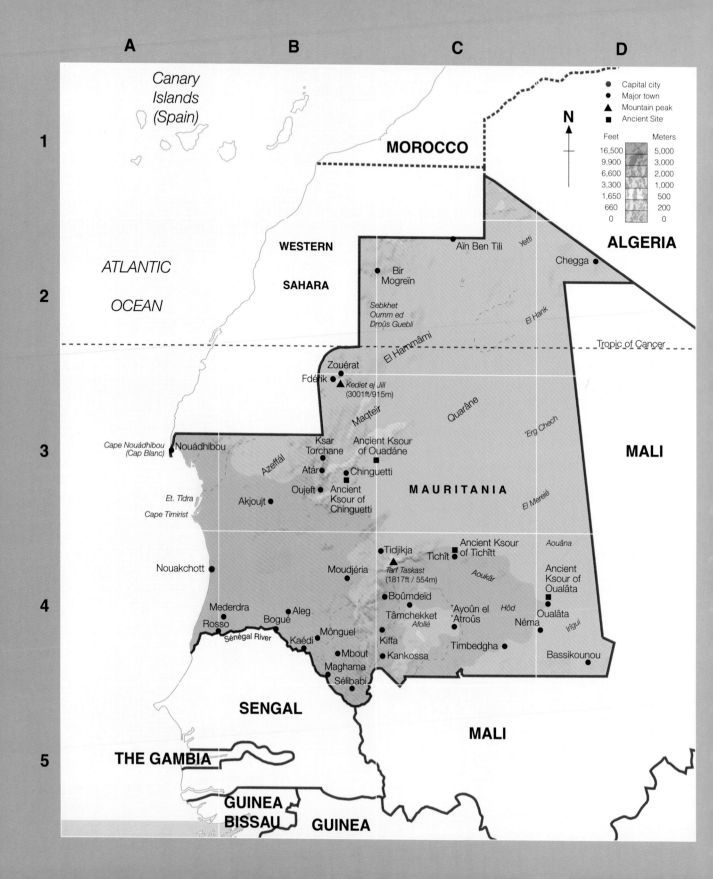

MAP OF MAURITANIA

ECONOMIC MAURITANIA

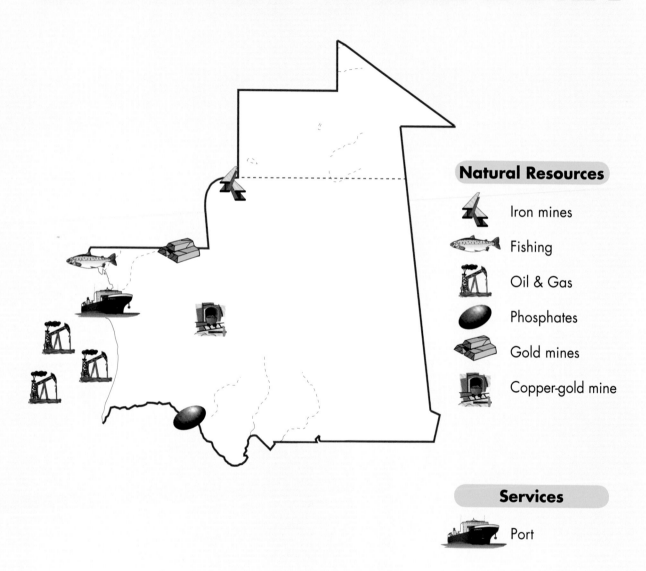

Natural Resources

Iron mines

Fishing

Oil & Gas

Phosphates

Gold mines

Copper-gold mine

Services

Port

ABOUT
THE ECONOMY

OVERVIEW

Despite its small population and considerable mineral and fishing resources, Mauritania remains one of the poorest countries in the world. Long years of military rule, a lack of planning for the future, and lasting droughts that have squeezed more than half the population into the cities, have all put a great strain on the economy. Foreign investors have been reluctant to put money into Mauritania because of the political instability. The rapid population growth has made it almost impossible for the economy to keep up with the peoples' needs. Because it is unable to produce enough food to feed its citizens, the country remains dependent on food aid from afar. Such aid makes up nearly one-quarter of the entire economy.

GROSS DOMESTIC PRODUCT (GDP)

$1.641 billion (2006 estimate)

GDP GROWTH

4 percent (2001 estimate)

GDP PER CAPITA

$2,600 (2006 estimate)

CURRENCY

Ouguiya $US1 = 268MRO

MAJOR IMPORTS

Food, machinery, petroleum products, consumer goods

MAJOR EXPORTS

Iron ore, fish, fish products, gold

WORKFORCE

786,000 (2001 estimate)

AGRICULTURAL PRODUCTS

Dates, millet sorghum, rice, corn, cattle, sheep

INFLATION

17.1 percent (2005 estimate)

UNEMPLOYMENT RATE

20 percent (2004 estimate)

POVERTY RATE

40 percent (2004 estimate)

MAJOR TRADING PARTNERS

France, United Kingdom, United States, China, Spain, Belgium, Germany, Japan (2005)

CULTURAL MAURITANIA

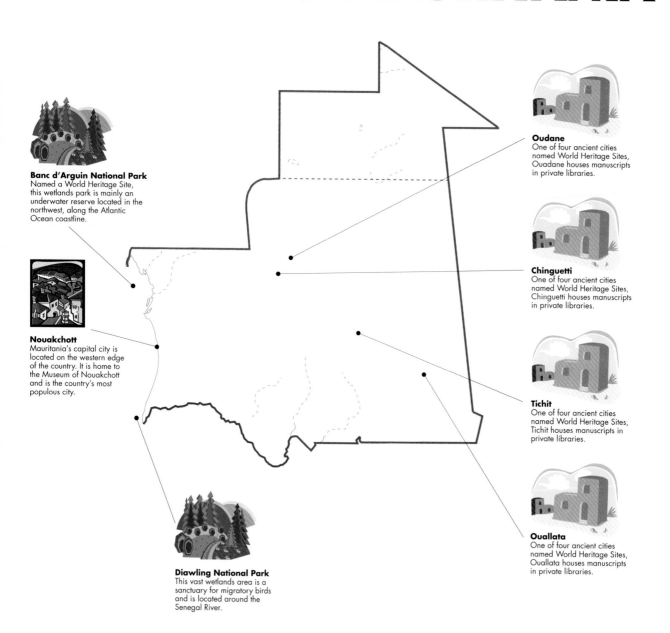

Banc d'Arguin National Park
Named a World Heritage Site, this wetlands park is mainly an underwater reserve located in the northwest, along the Atlantic Ocean coastline.

Nouakchott
Mauritania's capital city is located on the western edge of the country. It is home to the Museum of Nouakchott and is the country's most populous city.

Diawling National Park
This vast wetlands area is a sanctuary for migratory birds and is located around the Senegal River.

Oudane
One of four ancient cities named World Heritage Sites, Ouadane houses manuscripts in private libraries.

Chinguetti
One of four ancient cities named World Heritage Sites, Chinguetti houses manuscripts in private libraries.

Tichit
One of four ancient cities named World Heritage Sites, Tichit houses manuscripts in private libraries.

Ouallata
One of four ancient cities named World Heritage Sites, Ouallata houses manuscripts in private libraries.

ABOUT THE CULTURE

OFFICIAL NAME
Islamic Republic of Mauritania, Al Jumhuriyah al Islamiyah al Muritaniyah

NATIONAL FLAG
Green background with a yellow five-pointed star and a yellow crescent with the ends pointing upward; the color, the star, and the crescent are all symbolic of Islam

CAPITAL
Nouakchott

OTHER MAJOR CITIES
Nouadhibou, Aleg, Nema, Zouerat, Kaedi, Tidjika, Aioun, Kiffa, Atar, Selibay, Rosso, Akjoujt

ETHNIC GROUPS
Mixed Moor/black 40 percent, Moor 30 percent, black 30 percent

RELIGION
Islam

POPULATION
3,270,065 (2007 estimate)

LIFE EXPECTANCY
male 51.24 years; female: 55.85 years (2007 estimate)

LITERACY RATE
male 59.5%; female: 43.4% (2000 census)

NATIONAL HOLIDAY
November 28 (Independence from France in 1960)

TIME LINE

IN MAURITANIA	IN THE WORLD

8,000 B.C.
Ice Age ends.
4,000–3,000 B.C.
Agriculture established.
Circa 1200 B.C.
People settle into villages.

323 B.C.
Alexander the Great's empire stretches from Greece to India.

c. 200 A.D.
Camels introduced from Asia.
3rd–4th centuries
Berbers arrive from the north.
9th century
Group of Berbers form the Sanhadja Confederation.
11th–4th centuries
Islamic Almoravids take over the territory; Black Africans arrive; Yemeni Arabs move in from the north.

1000
The Chinese perfect gunpowder and begin to use it in warfare.
1100
Rise of the Incan Civilization in Peru.
1206–1368
Genghis Khan unifies the Mongols and starts conquest of the world. At its height, the Mongol Empire under Kublai Khan stretches from China to Persia and parts of Europe and Russia.

1441
Portuguese sailors reach Cap Blanc.
1455
The Portuguese establish a trading post at Arguin.

15th–16th centuries
Spanish, Dutch, and French nations claim the territory.
1644–74
The Mauritanian Thirty Years' War is fought between the Berbers and the Arabs.

1558–1603
Reign of Elizabeth I of England

1678
The French settle at the mouth of the Senegal River.

1776
U.S. Declaration of Independence

IN MAURITANIA	IN THE WORLD
	1789–99 The French Revolution
1815 The French are recognized as the colonial power in the region.	**1861** The U.S. Civil War begins.
	1869 The Suez Canal is opened.
1905 The French battle the Moors in Mauritania.	**1914** World War I begins.
1934 The French take over all of Mauritania.	
1939 World War II starts in Europe.	**1939** World War II begins.
	1941 Japan attacks Pearl Harbor.
	1945 The United States drops atomic bombs on Hiroshima and Nagasaki.
1960 Mauritania gains its independence from France.	**1949** The North Atlantic Treaty Organization (NATO) is formed.
	1966–69 The Chinese Cultural Revolution.
1975 Morocco organizes the Green March into Western Sahara to drive out Spain.	
1981 Mauritania bans slavery.	
	1986 Nuclear power disaster at Chernobyl in Ukraine
	1991 Breakup of the Soviet Union.
	1997 Hong Kong is returned to China.
	2001 Terrorists crash planes in New York, Washington D.C., and Pennsylvania.
2007 First civilian government elected; Sidi Ould Cheikh Abdallahi takes office.	**2003** War in Iraq begins.

GLOSSARY

alizé
Trade wind blowing from the east.

boubou
Loose garment worn by both men and women.

hajj
pilgrimage to Mecca.

harmattan
Desert wind from the Sahara.

ksar
Ancient fortified village.

malahfa
A long garment worn by Moorish women.

rifi
Wind blowing from the south.

FURTHER INFORMATION

BOOKS

Appiah, Kwame Anthony and Henry Louis Gates, Jr. Africana: *The Encyclopedia of the African and African American Experience.* New York: Basic Civitas Books, 2005.

Lonely Planet Travel Guide: *West Africa*, 6th edition., Hawthorn, Victoria, Australia: Lonely Planet Publications, 2006.

WEB SITES

Any Travels: Mauritania. Descriptions of Mauritania. http://www.anytravels.com/africa/mauritania

BBC News: Building a Road Across the Sahara. The Trans-Sahara Highway. http://news.bbc.co.uk/1/hi/world/africa/2161077.stm

Carter Center, The: Guinea Worm Eradication Program. http://cartercenter.org

Central Intelligence Agency World Factbook (select Mauritania from the country list). www.cia.gov/library/publications/the-world-factbook/index.html

Cotthem, Willem van. Desertification. The fight against desertification and other subjects in Mauritania and other drylands. http://desertification.wordpress.com/2007/06/27

Countries and Their Cultures: Culture of Mauritania. General background. http://www.everyculture.com/Ma-Ni/Mauritania.html

Country Studies: Islam in Mauritania. http://countrystudies.us/mauritania/38.htm

Go World Travel: On the Move in Mauritania. The iron ore train. http://www.goworldtravel.com/ex/aspx/articleGuid

Greentours Natural History Holidays: The Banc d'Arguin National Park. http://www.greentours.co.uk/holidays/Mauritania-birds.asp

Intelligence Agency World Factbook: LookLex—Mauritania. http://lexicorient.com/mauritania

Islam in Africa: Mauritania. http://www.islaminafrica.org/mauritania-h.htm

National Geographic: Running the Sahara. Describes the 2006 runners' journey across the Sahara in Mauritania. www.nationalgeographic.com/runningthesahara/map .html:

Tourism in Mauritania: Road of Hope. http://www.usmrbc.com/mainfile.php?%20lang=en&page=59

United Nations: Africa Renewal Magazine, July 2007. www.un.org/AR

BIBLIOGRAPHY

African News Agency: Afrol News. www.afrol.com

BBC News: In Pictures—Canary Isles Migrant Crisis. http://news.bbc.co.uk/1/hi/in_pictures/5299046.stm

Global Campaign for Education. Information on literacy rates. http://www.campaignforeducation.org/news/2007/newsletter_aug/aug_2007.htm

JCK Magazine, September 2007: "General background on Africa."

Mining Ministry of Mauritania; Mining Review magazine 2007; "Rio Narcea Gold Mines Mining conference in Cape Town", 2007.

New York Times, The. Background, many articles, including slavery in Mauritania, October 12, 1997; "Overfeeding girls": July 4, 2007.

International Red Cross/Red Crescent: Flooding and food aid needs. www.ifrc.org

Mondomix: All Colors of Music. http://dimi_mint_abba.mondomix.com/en/itw2719.htm

Offshore Technology: Chinguetti Oil Field. http://www.offshore-technology.com/projects/Chinguetti

UNICEF: Changing a Harmful Social Convention: Genital Mutilation/Cutting. www.unicef-irc.org/publications/pdf/fgm-gb-2005.pdf

Sunday Independent newspaper, South Africa; Cape Times newspaper, South Africa

United Nations News Service. Food aid as result of drought and locusts. www.un.org/apps/news/printnewsAr.asp?nid=13055

United Nations World Food Program http://www.wfp.org/english/?ModuleID=137&Key=2141

United States Department of State, Country Study: Mauritania www.state.gov/r/pa/ei/bgn/5467.htm

INDEX